# Worth Any Sacrifice

*personal encounters with angels*

# Worth Any Sacrifice

*personal encounters with angels*

*Jerry Gibson*

Edited by Victor W. Pearn

Busca, Inc.
Ithaca, New York

Busca, Inc.
P.O. Box 854
Ithaca, NY 14851
Ph: 607-546-4247
Fax: 607-546-4248
E-mail: info@buscainc.com
www.buscainc.com

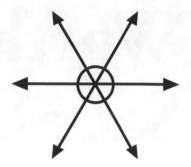

Cover art by Annie Hoff

First Edition

Printed in the United States of America

ISBN: 0-9666196-2-5

The publisher dedicates this project
to the beloved memory of Lloyd E. Prosperi.

# PRAYER

This book is written with a prayer that it may be a source of encouragement to all who read it and help them to realize that God's angels are watching over them.

# DEDICATION

This book is dedicated to Normadeene Gibson who is an example of what a Christian woman should be, as well as a faithful wife and helpmate to me, enduring untold hardships without a word of complaint, and a loving mother to our four children, Albert Joseph, Cynthia Charlotte, Jerry Jr. and Rebecca.

It is also dedicated to my mother Charlotte, "Lottie" who dedicated me to the service of the Lord before I was born.

# ACKNOWLEDGMENT

I would like to give a special honor to dear friends like Michael McFadden and Victor Pearn who spent countless hours helping to make this book as presentable as possible. There are many others that I have not mentioned but I know they realize what a blessing they've been to me.

Thank you and enjoy,
Jerry Gibson
March 22, 2002

# CONTENTS

# LIST OF ILLUSTRATIONS

# FOREWORD

Jerry Gibson has been my friend as well as one of my mentors for many years. I first met him when I was on the coaching staff of the University of Michigan's football team. He spoke to a prayer breakfast I had organized for several of my colleagues in Ann Arbor. He later renewed our fellowship after we both moved to Colorado. At our first meting he prayed with me in my office in the University of Colorado's football stadium, at which time I dedicated our football program to the Lord Jesus Christ. We went on to win the National Championship two years later. He was also with me at the meeting when Promise Keepers was born.

Jerry's book, *Worth Any Sacrifice,* reflects the kind of man that I strive to be. Like Isaiah of old, he is one of those rare individuals whose life demonstrates the fact that God's strong hand is upon them. His encounters with angels, as well as his relationships with friends and family, is a model for all to follow.

Jerry Gibson is a man dedicated to the service of Christ and his fellow man. He has spent over fifty years making disciples for Christ through his vast knowledge of the Bible. He has the wisdom God promises in James 1:5 if we seek it. He has been used by God to influence men and women around the world from Boulder, Colorado to Beijing, China as well as Minnesota and Africa. His outreach knows no boundaries.

Ecclesiastes 9:10 describes this man of God well. "Whatever your hand finds to do, do it with all your might, for in the grave where you will go there is neither working or planning nor knowledge or wisdom." Jerry has worked with all his might to further the kingdom of God. Whether young or old, educated or unlearned, a ruler or downcast, he knows no difference and sees all as those "for whom Christ died."

We thank the Lord daily for Jerry and the contribution he has made to so many lives. We pray that God will continue to raise up men just like him. We commend this book to you. Enjoy its content as you look upon a life that has influenced so many.

—Bill McCartney
Founder and C.E.O. of Promise Keepers

# PREFACE

"The angel of the Lord encamps all around those who fear him, and delivers them." Psalms 34:7

This book started out to be an attempt to share encounters our family has had with angels through the years; however, as we got into it, we realized that it should be expanded to include much more about family and friends, as well as kings and angels. In Book One we take you with us on our life's journey from 1926 to 1966. We have entitled this book, *Worth Any Sacrifice*. You will understand, the reason for this, when you get into the story. However, we will begin as we started, asking the question, "Will God deliver them that fear Him?"

The subject of "angels" has always intrigued the minds of men. From time to time, my wife Normadeene and I have shared our experiences with angels, with selected individuals. The sharing of some of these experiences has proven to be a source of comfort and encouragement to them. It gave them something to hang on to, during times of great trials and discouragement in their lives. The words of Paul in I Corinthians 10:13 have been a great source of inspiration to us through the years. Raising four children in the home of a preacher, college professor, foreign missionary, college president and campus minister, has proven to provide a number of situations and circumstances that seem to fall into the category of "beyond that which you are able," and "needing a way of escape." We have hesitated recounting our experiences publicly, as we did not want to give reason for the skeptic to fan the flames of his doubts about the power of

God in this world. We also, did not want the believer to question our integrity, and in some cases our sanity. We must admit that there were occasions when we did the latter ourselves. However, because so many people have urged us to share our experience, as a source of encouragement, this book is for the general public, believer and unbeliever alike. As best as we can recall, we will present our experiences with angels in chronological order in which we experienced them. We also want it to be known that there is nothing special about us. We are ordinary people with problems and temptations and trials that all of us face in our everyday lives. We are simply, like all who claim to be Christians, "sinners saved by His amazing grace." We seem to have needed a special measure of that grace more often than the average person. As we look back, God has never moved. He has always been there for us when we needed Him. The message we desire to get across in this book is that God is always there for you, too. His guardian angels are there to watch over you and your loved ones, and your deep concerns. You need but ask and He will be there with His angels.

# Biblical References to Angels

Angels are referred to both in The Old and New Testaments. It means literally "a messenger." It can refer to (1) A celestial being, a messenger of God, as in Genesis 2:47; Daniel 3:28 and Acts 12:8. (2) It can also refer to a minister or pastor of a church, as in Revelation 2:1. (3) On the negative side, it may refer to an evil, or fallen angel, as in Isaiah 12:13-15 in The Old Testament, and Matthew 25:41 in The New Testament.

The word translated "angel" in The Old Testament is the Hebrew "Malak." In The New Testament, the word is but a transliteration from the Greek "angelos." The first mention of angels in The Old Testament is in Genesis 16:7 in reference to God's dealing with Hagar, Abraham's concubine. Jacob's wrestling with an angel, as recorded in Genesis 32, is one of the most famous Biblical references to angels in The Old Testament. The first reference to angels in The New Testament is in Matthew 1:20 when an angel of the Lord spoke to Joseph and told him not to have any fear about taking Mary as his wife, as she had conceived by The Holy Spirit.

We do not intend for this book to be a scholarly discourse, but rather to be a source of inspiration.

*Part I*

ANGELS IN THE BIBLE
AND OUR FIRST ENCOUNTER

# Chapter I
## OUR FIRST ENCOUNTER

"For he will give his angels charge concerning you, to guard you in all of
your way. THEY WILL BEAR YOU UP IN THEIR HANDS. . . ." Psalms
91:11

It happened the first time when I was just four years old. Dad had received his long waited for World War I bonus. During the school year he
was a school teacher and coach. He needed money to support our family
during the summer months. At that time our family consisted of my father and mother, my three older sisters and myself. Dad decided to use his
bonus money to study ballet in Chicago, under the then famous Pavily
O'Crensky. He was a man for whom Dad had great respect and admiration. Dad planned on teaching ballet during the summer months in our
home in Minneapolis, Minnesota.

Due to our limited finances, we could not afford to live in a hotel in
the Chicago area while Dad attended his classes. Dad rented a canvas covered cabin near Lake Michigan close to the Des Plaines river. It was the
closest thing to "camping out" without living in a tent.

It was a beautiful, cool, summer evening when it happened. It had
rained all day long. There was a special fresh fragrance in the air, like often
after a summer rain. My three older sisters, Lillian, Billie, and Millie decided to go on an exploration trip in the vicinity of the campground. As
mentioned earlier, the Des Plaines river was near by, along with many
other interesting things that fascinated young minds. However, the last
thing they wanted was to have their little brother "Junior," which I was
called at that time in my young life, tagging along. I had other ideas. I was

not about to let them go without me. I was not going to miss out on this exciting adventure. Who knows, we might discover some buried treasure, hidden by pirates, who carried it in from Lake Michigan, and were not able to come back to retrieve it.

The girls started to run, hoping to lose me. But I was a fast little guy. I kept right up with them. Millie, my sister closest to my age, had a pretty, little, red rubber ball. I liked that little red rubber ball very much. She was not willing to part with it, though. I must admit, that even at that young age, I was guilty of the sin of covetousness. I had earlier begged Millie to let me have her ball. Now her chance came to get rid of her "tag along" little brother. She spotted, what seemed to her to be a shallow pool of water. It was completely covered over by a film of green moss and algae. It looked like solid ground to me. She threw her pretty little red rubber ball into the middle of the pool and ran off with her two older sisters. As much as I desired to share the girl's adventure, I wanted the pretty little, red rubber ball more. So, like a flash, without any thought of peril, I attempted to walk on water to retrieve the ball. The rain had filled the pool to the brim. I found myself in water over my head. I started to sink under the green blanket of slimy moss, that held up that pretty little red rubber ball. I went under the slimy water, and started to thrash around for my life! I had already swallowed, what seemed to me, to be half of the water in the pool. I came up gasping for air. Then it happened! I had my first encounter with an angel. Just as I started to sink under that slimy water for a second time, "a peace that passes understanding" overwhelmed my being. I felt a strong sure hand lift me up out of that slimy pit of water, and place my feet safely on solid ground. I looked to see who had come to my help me. There was nobody there but me. My angel had come to rescue me.

As I look back in retrospect, I should have been concerned about my mother's reaction to seeing me wet and dirty, covered with the green moss and slime from the pond. She had dressed me in a little white linen suit, and instructed me to try to not get too dirty. Somehow, that spirit of peace never left me. I felt no fear from my mother, and she showed no anger. Only comforting words came from her lips. It was as though she knew what had happened. I can remember, as though it was yesterday, Mom putting clean pajamas on me, and tucking me into the clean folds of the cool blankets on the cot where I was sleeping. She kissed me goodnight, after saying a short prayer. I slept well that night knowing that something very special had happened to me. My angel was watching over me.

# Chapter II
## Motorcycle Angel

"He gives power to the faint; and to them that have no might he increases
strength." Isaiah 40:29

Many years passed before I had another encounter with "My angel."
It happened shortly before I was shipped out to the South Pacific, during
the Second World War.

It was early in 1944. Due to the number of times our family moved
when I was a young boy, I was held back a year when I was in third grade.
As a result, many of my closest friends were a year ahead of me, and had
graduated from high school, and had entered the military. They had either
been drafted, or had enlisted in the branch of the service they preferred. In
the middle of my junior year of high school, I asked permission from my
parents to quit school and join the Navy. I was a very patriotic young man,
and desired to follow the path of those who went before me, to bring the
war with Germany, Italy and Japan to a victorious end. After much per-
suasion, they reluctantly gave their consent. I left for duty in the Navy
before the school year ended. I was sent to school in Jacksonville, Florida,
the very place where I was born. I was sent there to be trained to become
an Aviation Electronic Technician. I loved math, and was good at solving
equations, so I breezed through the classes. Upon graduating from The
Naval Aviation Technical Training Center, I expected to receive a leave
before being shipped out. But that is not what happened. Due to the
many Naval battles that were taking place, there was an urgent need for
men with my particular skills, to help keep our naval aircraft in the air. I
received orders to report immediately to Camp Kearney, near San Diego,

California. It took a week for our troop transport train to travel from the East to the West Coast. We didn't think we would ever get through Texas. Soon after arriving in California, we transferred from Camp Kearney to Camp Elliot. Then, to our dismay, we received orders to be shipped to an unknown destination before receiving a much needed, and well deserved leave. We had not been home since boot camp, and were very homesick. If we could just see our parents, and friends back home, we would be ready to go wherever we were needed.

We were told we could have a weekend pass, to do whatever we desired. However, we were to be back on the base in time to ship out to our new assignment. To further complicate the situation, our pay records had not yet caught up with us, so, the only money we would have for the weekend liberty, would be what we had managed to save from our last pay check. I had not managed to save a penny. I was dead broke!

I soon found out that many of my fellow sailors were in the same boat. One of them told me that a shuttle bus would take us free of charge to the Main Gate. From there we could walk to the highway. We could hitchhike south to San Diego, or north to Los Angeles. He had family in San Diego who would take care of his needs if he could get to them. A flash of hope came into my mind. My sister, Millie was working at The Burbank Theater in Los Angeles. I was sure that if I could find her, I would be able to satisfy two, very urgent needs in my life. I would be able to borrow enough money from Millie to tide me over until I received my pay. But most important, I would be able to spend some time with a member of my immediate family before being shipped overseas. I was a very lonely and homesick, young man. The thought of seeing Millie really brought joy and hope into my heart.

Early Saturday morning, I caught the shuttle bus down to the Main Gate. I then briskly walked to the highway which I thought would take me to Los Angeles, and a blessed reunion with my sister Millie. I thought I had started plenty early. But when I got to the highway, soldiers, sailors, Marines, Wacs and Waves were already lining the sides of the road, all seeking to find rides to Los Angeles or San Diego. I took my place in line. It was about 7:30 A.M. I thought the line would soon grow shorter in front of me, and I would soon be able to hitch a ride. However, the line grew longer in front of me, and behind me. By 2:30 P.M. that afternoon,

I was becoming very discouraged, and a little bitter.

A car would pull up, and the driver would shout, "I'll take you to Los Angeles for five dollars." People would scurry to take advantage of the offer. But I didn't have five dollars. I didn't even have a penny. Things began to look very hopeless for me. As I stood there, feeling very sorry for myself, suddenly I remembered how my mother told me to pray to God if I ever found myself in a crisis situation. She also told me that she was praying for me without ceasing. She said she claimed the promises of The Ninety-first Psalm, that God would surround me with His guardian angels. She urged me to attend the chapel service on the base on Sunday mornings. She also suggested that it wouldn't do any harm for me to offer a few prayers of my own.

Up until that time, I had satisfied the first part of her wishes. I had attended the chapel services on the base in Jacksonville. However, I had never offered an audible prayer, or as far as that goes, an inaudible prayer in my life. I was confident that her prayers would be enough to take care of me. I didn't think that The Great God Almighty had time in His busy schedule, with the war going on and everything, to hear the prayers of a little, insignificant, Second Class Seaman. That is what I was at the time all of this was happening. I started to feel even more sorry for myself. I was angry at my mother for telling me God was hearing her prayers, and would take care of me. And I was angry at God for treating me this way. The longer I stood there, the more I felt sorry for myself, and the angrier I got at both my mother and God. I was having one gigantic "pity party." And the line of soldiers, sailors, Marines, Wacs and Waves grew longer in front of me, and behind me. I was certain I was not going to see Millie in Los Angeles. I was never going to get a ride. I was going to have to walk back to the Naval base. But worst of all, I was going to be shipped overseas without having seen any of my family or loved ones. Loneliness and hopelessness overwhelmed me!

Then, once again, I remembered my mother's words. She said, "If you ever find yourself in trouble, just ask God, and He will help you." I was in deep trouble. I didn't think I could last very long overseas, on some God forsaken island, with the loneliness and homesickness I was feeling. I decided to take Mom's advice, and test the strength of her faith in God. She was so sure He was hearing her prayers, and assured me, He would hear my prayers, too.

As I mentioned earlier, I had never prayed before, other than the prayers we had memorized for the dinner table, or "the now I lay me down to sleep" prayer we said with Mom when we were little children, when she tucked us into bed. The situation in which I found myself, called for some very serious praying. The prayer I uttered that afternoon, was more in the form of "a bargain" than a petition. I reminded God of my mother's steadfast faith in Him, and the promises and assurances she had made to me on His behalf. I reminded Him how terrible it would be for me to be shipped overseas without seeing at least one of my loved ones, namely my sister Millie. I then made a promise to Him. If He would help me get a ride to Los Angeles, and enable me to spend some time with my sister, then I will seriously consider being His servant. But if He did not help me out of my dier predicament, I would tell my mother to stop praying for me, because the God in whom she puts so much trust is not real, and I didn't want her to mention His name to me again. No sooner had I finished that prayer, I heard a voice saying, "Are you particular how you ride?" I looked up, and there sat a man on a motorcycle. I looked at the line of hitch hikers that had grown longer in front of me, and behind me. I was in a state of shock! I kept thinking of the prayer I had just prayed, and the bargain I had made with God. The man on the motorcycle didn't even ask me where he should take me. He seemed to already know. That feeling of peace once again flooded my soul. Not a word was said. He took me right to the main entrance of The Burbank Theater where Millie was working.

I got off the motorcycle, after what was my first motorcycle ride, sore, but grateful. I turned to thank him. He and the motorcycle were gone.

I had a wonderful time with Millie that weekend. But all of the time I kept thinking about the strange man on the motorcycle. I kept asking myself, why did he pass everyone else, most of whom had some money, and stop by me. I was now ready, I thought, for whatever was in store for me in The South Pacific. Unfortunately, I soon forgot the promise I had made to God. It would not be long before another crisis situation came into my life, and I remembered it.

## Chapter III
## LOTTIE

*Lottie as a little girl*

On a hot and humid summer night, a bright star hovered over the farmhouse of Raymond and Evelyn King. It was August 11, 1901. On this night a child was born whose birth would effect the lives of many, for all eternity. For this was the night Charlotte King, affectionately known as Lottie, was born into this world. The world would never be the same, because she affected the lives of all with whom she came into contact. It was said of the prototype of all heroes, Achilles, "He recognized his destiny in life, and he lived his life!" Very few people can say that of themselves. Lottie King was one of those rare individuals, who recognized her destiny, and fulfilled it. It has well been said, "The history of the world is the history of great men and women. They come to us like lightning from the sky. They ignite us! Then, we too, begin to glow."

I thought it appropriate to introduce Lottie into this story, due to the tremendous influence she had on my life. And also because of the providential way her life was spared, by her guardian angel, in order to bring me into this world.

Lottie was one of ten children born into the Raymond King family. She idolized her older brothers, and attempted to imitate them in whatever way possible. On one such occasion, she played follow-the-leader with them. They climbed on the roof of their barn. She lost her footing, and was falling fifty feet to the ground, when a hand reached out, and hung her neatly on a harness hook by a rib just below her heart. Her brothers were sure she was dead. However, she came out of that experience with

*Jerry's mother and father, Lottie and Gerald, with Normadeene and their great-granddaughter Missy many years later*

just a small scar to remind her, and all who knew her, that she must have a special mission to accomplish in this life. Her angel had come to her rescue.

One afternoon, Lottie's father was crushing the clods that covered his Kansas wheat farm. He was driving a huge steam roller that weighed several thousand pounds. It had large metal wheels, and an even larger metal roller that would crush the clods of dirt. Lottie idolized her father, and wanted to be with him whenever possible. She followed him around like a puppy dog. Lottie was running along side of that big machine, when she tripped and fell into the path of those big iron wheels, and that large metal roller. It ran right over her little body! Her father jumped off of the machine, and ran screaming into the house, "Lottie is dead! Lottie is dead!" He then returned and backed the huge machine off of her frail little body. But to his relief, she was not dead! She had only suffered a broken collar bone. It was a miracle!

Lottie was born into this world on Sunday, August 11, 1901. She was called home to glory, on Sunday, August 11, 1991, on her ninetieth birthday. As I stood by her bedside, during the final hours of her life, she told me that before I was born, she had prayed to God that she would have a son, and someday, he would become a preacher of the Gospel. She said that she believed the reason her life was spared, and she was able to give birth to eight children, was that at least one of them would grow up to be a preacher of the Gospel. She went on to say, her guardian angel protected her so that she could give birth to me. Her words helped me to understand many of the things that I share with you in this book.

## Chapter IV
### ANGELS AT SEA

"A thousand shall fall at thy side, and ten thousand at thy right hand; but it shall not come near thee." Psalms 91:7

We shipped out of North Island Naval Air Base on a cloudy Monday morning. We were headed for Pearl Harbor on *The U.S.S. Norton Sound,* the largest seaplane tender in the world. It took us seven days to make the voyage from San Diego to Hawaii. I had my first experience with sea-sickness during those seven days. At first I thought I was going to die. Then, I was afraid I would not die. The sea was rough, and even though our ship was a large vessel, it was tossed about on the mountainous waves as though it were a tooth pick. I didn't get sick right away. It wasn't until the sailors all around me got sick, that the sound of men vomiting, and the smell that accompanied their vomiting got to me. It was a great relief to me to finally dock in Pearl Harbor. I remember the tragic sight of many of our ships lying sunk in the harbor. The memory of what I saw that day came back to me vividly some forty years later, when I revisited the site with Normadeene.

After spending several weeks in Pearl Harbor, we finally received our orders to ship out to an unknown destination in the South Pacific. I was assigned to LST 895, a small naval landing craft that was used to take troops ashore at the time of sea to land invasions. I can recall that several of them had large pontoons, as well as other equipment strapped to their sides. They were the components of what was to become the largest float-ing dry dock in the world. Once it was in operating order, we would no longer have to send our damaged vessels all of the way back to Pearl Harbor or San Francisco for necessary repairs. We could do it right there in the harbor of Guam. Guam is where our flotilla of ships was heading. However, we had a forty-two day voyage ahead of us. It was a voyage that proved to be very dangerous, as well as very frightening. We were tired and edgy. We were anxious to place our feet on dry ground. The seas had been very rough. The waves mounted up into the heavens, and then went down into the depths. They tossed our little vessel around, as suggested earlier on our trip to Hawaii, the swells raged so severe, they broke one of our vessels in half. The large pontoons the LST was carrying for the dry dock, is all that kept both halves afloat.

We finally reached the Marshal Islands. We docked at Eniwetok Harbor, and were allowed to go ashore. It was a great relief to be on dry land again. We were hot and thirsty. When we got on shore, we immediately went to the beer gardens, where we were given warm cans of Griesedieck beer and cans of salted Spanish peanuts. We drank down the beer and gobbled down the salted peanuts like they were a delicious Thanksgiving dinner. The island was small, dry and barren. It was strategically located in the South Pacific, though. It was not far from the Japanese occupied island of Truk.

We returned to our LST that night, and gathered down in the hold of the little vessel to watch an old Clark Gable movie. Then it happened! All hell broke loose! The P.A. system began to shout, "All hands man your battle stations! Man your battle stations! General quarters! Man your battle stations!" The sound of the sirens and other warning systems were deafening! The Japanese were attacking, and we were stuck down in the hold of our LST with only two little hatches for exits. We were trapped, with no other way to get out. Everyone made a mad scramble for those two little hatches! It was pure bedlam! Everyone was panicking and yelling,"Let me out of here!" Those that made it to the top first had already started to man our fifty caliber guns. We could hear the steady ACK! ACK! ACK! Then we would hear an occasional BOOM! BOOM! BOOM! That came from our larger guns. We could hear the sound of our SB2C Hell Divers and F6F Hell Cats dog fighting with the Japanese Zeros and Betties. We could hear the screaming sound of bombs that fell dangerously close to our little ship. We were praying that one of those bombs would not score a hit on our little vessel while we were still trapped below. I was far away from either of the two escape hatches, and there were many frightened sailors between me and the hatches. I thought, this is it! I'm never going to make it out of here alive.

Then, as it happened so long ago at that campsite near Chicago, I felt a strong hand reach down and grab me. It carried me over the bodies of the sailors in front of me, and pushed me up the ladder to the hatch. I found myself safe on deck. At that moment, the "All clear" sounded. I had experienced another encounter with my angel.

# Chapter V
## ON THE ROCK

I spent nearly eighteen months on the Island of Guam. For most of that time, I was the only single man living in a Quonset hut with thirty married men. That proved to be a very interesting experience. Some of them had some extremely difficult experiences. I will never forget the day when Eddy Mean, one of the older men in our outfit, received a "Dear John" letter from his wife. Eddy grew old over night. Somehow, my mother managed to get a letter off to me at least once a week during all of the time

*Jerry on Guam in 1945*

I was on Guam. However, it took the mail two months to reach us after we left Hawaii. Included in my mail from my mother was a birthday cake. The frosting had become like cement. I mistakenly left it on my bed when I went back to the revetments to work on aircraft. I came back late at night, completely exhausted. I had forgotten about the birthday cake. I crawled into my cot and was immediately covered by little red fire ants. They had consumed the birthday cake, and had eaten most of my blanket and sheets. They now began to eat on me. I made the quickest dash to our makeshift shower that I had ever made. For days after, I kept feeling those ants eating on my body. I itched all over, and I scratched continually.

*Jerry on Guam drinking water from a "blister bag" container*

Shortly after landing on Guam, we were sleeping in tents in the jungle along side of the airstrip we had captured from the Japanese. The Sea Bees had bulldozed the Japanese aircraft off the bomb-pocked runway, and laid portable landing strips on the old Japanese runway. It was a while before the Sea Bees were able to build the Quonset huts we would live in. I vividly remember how when we let down the tent flap, a huge centipede came scurrying out of the tent flap and ran down the side of my arm. Fortunately, my arm was covered with my dungaree shirt, as the centipedes on that island were extremely poisonous, and everywhere one of their legs come into contact with your skin it would cause severe infection. Eddie Meaon, Bill Prince and Jack Fry were in the tent with me.

It happened the very first night we were in that tent. Somehow, we got to talking about how easy it would be for a "Jap," as we referred to the enemy, to sneak into our tent while we were sleeping and slit our throats. I believe the older men were trying to scare me. They succeeded, but in the process managed to scare themselves. Each of us had a thirty caliber carbine, as well as a large machete knife. We all slept with them under our pillows. It took a long time for any of us to fall asleep that night, even though we were all exhausted from the rigors of landing and setting up our base on Guam.

At about mid-night I woke up from a fitful sleep to the noise of Eddie Meaon in a death struggle with someone or something. He was moaning over and over, "Uh! Uh! Uh! Uh!" I was sure a Japanese had come into our tent, and that Eddie was having a death struggle with him.

*Japanese two-man submarine captured off Guam*

I thought my heart would beat out of my chest, and that the "Jap" would hear it and get me next. I looked, and there stood a shadowy white figure. Eddy was grappling with it. I managed to get my flashlight out and shine it in that direction. At that instant, the figure of that man was gone. I jumped out of bed with the other men in our tent following. Eddy was screaming hysterically. We shook him, and slapped him, and told him to that all was well.

By that time, the rest of our outfit had heard the commotion. The Corporal of the Guard came running over to our tent and yelled, "What's going on?" We said, "Nothing, Eddy has just had a bad dream." And we dismissed it with that. However, I knew better. For a brief moment I had looked into the face of that shadowy white figure Eddy had been wrestling with. As I look back, I am now convinced that God had sent that angel to let us know that what He said in Psalms 91 is true. "A thousand may fall at your side, and ten thousand at your right hand, but it shall not come near you. . . . For He shall give His angels charge over you." Psalms 91:7-11. Eddy was never the same after that. But neither was I. Once again I had that feeling of peace that I had experienced so long ago when I felt that strong hand lift me out of that muddy pit and placed my feet on dry land. Many things happened during those eighteen months that followed while I was on Guam.

I am confident that I would never have returned safely to civilian life, had it not been for my guardian angel watching over me. Before closing this chapter, I want to recount an experience that happened just shortly before I left Guam to come back to the States that is significant. Somehow, I almost forgot to relate it to you. It enabled me to return to America and some day fifty years later write this book about my experience with angels. After the war was over, with the bombing of Hiroshima and Nagasaki, I was left in charge of many of the everyday duties of the electricians from CASU 12 (Combat Service Unit 12) which I was a member. One of my duties was to see to it that the auxiliary batteries for the radio and radar shacks were always fully charged and ready for any emergency that might occur. We had been hit be several power outages when hurricanes passed over Guam. On a very hot afternoon, just before I was to get off duty, I decided to check the batteries in the generator room. For some reason or other I did not have my mind on what I was doing. I was very hot and sweaty, and very tired. I entered the generator room with a hydrometer in my hand and leaned over to take the caps off of the large batteries that were constantly being charged by large generators. I forgot the big knife switches that I was supposed to open before checking the batteries. I leaned down with my wet body on those large knife switches that held several thousand volts of electricity. I felt the jolt of electricity hit my bare arm. Because of the type of current, I should have stuck right to those big copper switches and been burned alive right then and there. However, the moment my arm hit the knife switches, somebody hit my arm hard and threw me away from the switches. I fell to the floor and looked for the person who had just saved my life. There was nobody there but me. My arm was aching and became black and blue and badly bruised. I realized that once again my guardian angel had saved my life.

## Chapter VI
## HOME AT LAST

In the wee hours of the morning, we gathered on the "grinder" for bag inspection before leaving for the harbor and boarding the *U.S.S Hermitage*, which was going to take us home by way of what was then called "The Great Circle Route." The *Hermitage* was a converted Italian luxury liner that was being used to transport troops back to the States. We had been up all night, and then forced to empty our sea bags out onto the asphalt surface of the grinder for inspection. It was surprising what many of the sailors intended to take back home with them. Some had packed live ammunition with their other belongings. One man had packed a live hand grenade in his duffel bag. When I saw that, I realized why the inspection was necessary. Several hours later we climbed the steep ladder from our motor launch and were whistled on board that huge vessel. I was assigned a bunk as far down in the hold as possible, in the F compartment.

The bunks were stacked six high, with barely enough room to roll over, as they were spaced so close together. At first nobody minded, because we were going home! We could put up with anything, as long as we eventually got back to the States. That is, almost anything. We had not anticipated that most of those down in that furthest compartment below decks would become sea sick and vomit all over the deck as well as anyone whose bunk was below them. The heat was stifling, and along with the smell of vomit, everyone eventually became deathly sick. At first you were afraid you were going to die, as mentioned before. Then you were afraid you would not die. That went on for several days. The sea was particularly rough. Even though the *Hermitage* was a very large ship, it was tossed about by mountainous waves. The rougher the sea got, the sicker everyone became. We were out to sea about four days when we got word that a

*Jerry and Mr. R. Bruce Reinecker when Jerry was 12*

Destroyer was trying to locate our ship so that they could transfer a sailor to our ship, who was near death with appendicitis. The stormy raging sea had not let up at all, and we wondered how they would manage the transfer of that sick sailor from the Destroyer to our ship. But our first order of business was for the two ships to locate each other under conditions that were far from being ideal. The rain was coming down so hard, and the waves were tossing our ship so severely that we could not see more than a few feet. All at once, a bow of a ship loomed up just below where I was standing. It was too late to avoid a collision! The sound was deafening as the bow of the Destroyer plowed through the side of our ship and tore a gaping hole in her own bow!

As I said, I was standing right in front of where the Destroyer hit us. Once again, I was sure I would not get back home, as I found myself flung backward toward the bulkhead of our ship. I waited to hit the steel plates of the bulkhead, but instead, I felt a cushion around my body, and I was softly placed on the deck beside the ship's bulkhead. After several

*Jerry conferring a doctor's degree on Bruce Reinecker some fifty years later*

hours of emergency repairs on both of our vessels, the attempt to transfer the sick sailor to our ship was abandoned. I always wondered what happened to him. However, I knew that something very special had happened to me again. My guardian angel had once again saved my life. I immediately went down into the hold of that ship and recounted the experience in my diary. I wrote a letter to my mother that night telling her that God had heard and answered her prayers for me.

Several days later, after the sea was calm, I had one of the most wonderful and exciting experiences of my life. Our ship went under The Golden Gate Bridge in San Francisco Harbor, and passed by what was then Alcatraz, and docked at Treasure Island. As we went under that beautiful bridge, we all tossed our hats into the air and let out a tremendous cheer! We were home at last.

*Part II*

A TRUE STORY ABOUT ANGELS

## Chapter VII
## THE TURNING POINT

Our ship docked at Treasure Island, one of the main Naval bases in Northern California. I spent two weeks there mostly on liberty, while waiting to be processed out of the service. Due to the fact that my family had moved from Minnesota to California while I was still on Guam, I decided to process out of the Navy in California, rather than travel back to St.Paul, Minnesota where I had enlisted. The Navy paid me for the cost of travel back to Minnesota, so I had a goodly amount of money left over after buying my plane ticket to Los Angeles, where my parents were then residing. I received my discharge from the Navy on June 4, 1946. My reunion with my father and mother and brothers and sisters was a sweet one. I spent the next few weeks getting used to being a civilian once again.

That summer I went to live with my sister and brother-in-law, Lil and Jud. Jud had been discharged from the Marine Corps a few months before I got back to the States. He was one of the Marines on Iwo Jima where the famous raising of the flag took place on Mount Suribachi. Jud had written a letter to me from a fox hole near where the fierce fighting took place, a place where many American and Japanese men lost their lives. Jud expressed his fear in that letter that he might never get out of there alive. He did get out. And he got home safe and sound. His story is a courageous one. He had lost his Commission in the Marine Corps due to ground looping his training plane while he was stationed at Cherry

Point, North Carolina. He immediately offered his services to our country by becoming an enlisted man in the Marines. Not many men could have survived the humbling experience Jud went through. Lil and Jud opened both their hearts and home to me. Jud and I got a job working for Union Carbide and Carbon that summer. The foreman on our job must have seen something special in me, as he kept urging me to quit the job, and take advantage of The G.I. Bill, and further my education. It is interesting to note that our youngest son, "G.A." worked for that same company in Danbury, Connecticut. That seems to me to be a strange coincidence, after so many years.

I decided to take the advice of the foreman, and enrolled in San Bernardino Valley College. My parents had moved to Muscoy, a small suburb of San Bernardino. I could not afford to live away from home, so I moved in with them. At that time, I did not have any real sense of purpose for my life. Due to the fact that my father had been a coach and teacher, I decided to major in Physical Education, and perhaps follow his footsteps. I also had in the back of my mind becoming a golf professional, as golf had played a major roll in my life during my teens. I had the privilege of caddying for Walter Hagan, one of golf's most famous players. I also was the caddie for Bruce Reinecker, the founder and President of National School Studios, that led the photography industry in taking school photos. It is known today as Life Touch International based in Minneapolis, Minnesota. An interesting side light, in regard to Bruce Reinecker, is the fact that al-

*Normadeene and her mother, Hattie Pletcher, standing by Me Too*

most fifty years from the time I was his caddie, I had the privilege of presenting my former boss with an Honorary Doctor of Humanities Degree from Mid-South Christian College where I was the President for seven years.

College classroom work was very easy for me. I did not have to spend much time studying, and was on the honor roll after the first semester. I decided to try out for the golf team. Coach Opp, the golf coach, was a close friend of my father, as he was also the football coach and track coach, the same as my father was during his coaching days. Our golf team won the Western Junior College Championship that Spring. I was the number two man on the team behind Dick McCook, who was a fine young man and an excellent golfer. He transferred to Stanford, and I was elected Captain of the Golf Team. I also moved up to the number one position.

Several members of our championship golf team, and me, decided to celebrate our golf championship by having a "beer bust" down at the beach. Several girls from college agreed to join in with us in our celebration. We were to bring along what were then called "picnics" of beer. They were large oversized bottles. As I look back, I realize how empty our lives were at that time, and how sad it was that we thought that happiness could be obtained out of a bottle. I loaded my 1929 Chevrolet coupe with picnic supplies and beer, and started off on a Sunday morning to meet my beer drinking buddies and head for the beach. I was very proud of that little Chevy coupe, as I had upholstered it in red corduroy, thinking that would serve to attract girls. As I drove down E Street in San Bernardino, I noticed a motor cycle cop out of my rear view mirror. I then noticed that he was motioning for me to pull over to the side of he road. I was wearing one of my "ruptured duck" pins that designated I was a World War II veteran. I thought that would make me less liable to receive a traffic citation. I soon found out how wrong I was. The officer roared at me, "The lens on your tail light is missing!" I told him that I realized that, and had been trying to find one. However, due to the war, it was almost impossible to find spare parts of any kind. He then proceeded to walk around the front of my classic vehicle, and then roared again, "The lens on your left front headlight is also missing!" Once again I attempted to explain to the fuming officer that I had been trying to find a headlight lens. He then opened the driver's side door of the car, and placed his hand on the brake pedal, and pushed it all of the way to the floorboard. They were supposed to be mechanical brakes. He then asked me to test out my horn. I had a piece of wire that I would ground on the steering post. It went, Yooga! Yooga! Yooga! The officer then roared once more, "Young man, I am going to give you a ticket just for having this car!" He proceeded to write me out a ticket, and told me to get the necessary repairs within the next ten days, or keep my vehicle off the road.

I was deeply hurt. He had bruised my tender feelings for my wonderful car. How could he treat a veteran that way, I grumbled to myself. Then as I proceeded further down E Street. A strange thing happened. I glanced over the left side of the street and saw a church with a sign saying, Fourteenth and E Church of Christ, a nondenominational Christian Church. I had never heard of a nondenominational church before. At that instance something or some unseen force grabbed hold of my steering wheel and forced me to the curb across from that church. I then found myself walking up the stairs and on into the church building. The services were already in progress. I spotted the only vacant seat, I could see, next to the aisle. Trying not to be noticed, I slipped into that open seat. Little did I realize that this would be *the "turning point" in my life.* I later found out that I was sitting by Russell Boatman and his brother Don Earl Boatman, both who were to become my very close friends. The preacher, Herold E. Hossom, a graduate of Cincinnati Bible Seminary, seemed to forget about everyone else in the audience, and preached right at me. He preached a simple but powerful message on the Gospel of Jesus Christ. He then gave an invitation for people to make a decision based on his message and accept Jesus Christ as their Lord and Savior. I had never made such a decision. In fact, I had never been in a church that offered such an invitation. I then found myself rushing to the front of that sanctuary, eager to confess my new found faith in Jesus the Christ, the Son of the Living God. Preacher Hossom then told me that I must be baptized. He said I should be immersed in the baptistry at the back of the speaker's platform. I had never witnessed a baptism, let alone one by immersion. I protested that I had been baptized in a Methodist Church in Wisconsin when I was a baby. He went to explain that that was for my parents to commit themselves to raising me in a Christian home, and now as a result, I was to be baptized on the basis of my own personal faith in Jesus Christ. In short, he said,

"God has no grandchildren." He proceeded to tell me that Jesus set the example for this, and commanded us to follow His example. I knew what he said was true, but I told him I would like to think about it more. He agreed that I should do so. A week later I returned to the church with two or three other members of my family, and we were baptized into Christ that morning.

We returned for the Sunday evening evangelistic hour. Herold Hossom delivered another powerful sermon challenging those present to commit themselves to specialized service for our Lord. He closed the service by giving an invitation for Full Time Specialized Service. At first I did not think he was including me in that invitation. However, he kept looking at me. As I pondered this frightening invitation, I began to think about the fact that there must be hundreds of young people, who like me, were wandering aimlessly through life without any real purpose or sense of direction in their lives. Who if they could hear the sweet Gospel message just once, just like I had heard it, would respond to it, just as I had responded. Once again I found myself walking down the aisle, along with more than a dozen young men and women, presenting ourselves to Jesus for Specialized Christian Service. When I made the announcement of my decision, most of my family seemed surprised. However, my mother had long ago prayed, as I mentioned earlier in this book, that one of her sons would one day be a preacher. Her prayers were doubly answered, as my brother Harlow is also an ordained minister of the Gospel. She further rejoiced when she learned that our oldest son, Albert Joseph also committed himself to become a minister of the Gospel. Coach Opp, my golf coach and football coach, was the most upset by my decision. I was leaving his Golf Team of which I was the Captain and number one man, and also his football team where I was one of his quarterbacks. Like many others, he didn't realize that I was giving up "that which I could not keep" in exchange for "that which I could not lose." I traded my beautiful little 1929 Chevrolet coupe for a 1936 Chevrolet coupe. I realize now that it was "my angel" that forced that 1929 Chevrolet coupe to the curb and made possible "the turning point in my life."

## Chapter VIII
## ME TOO

Aweek later, half of those who had made a commitment that Sunday evening, left San Bernardino for Cincinnati Bible Seminary, and the other half, including me, for Minnesota Bible College in Minneapolis, Minne-

*Jerry in Muscoy, near San Bernardino, just after mustering out of the Navy*

sota. Russell E. Boatman was the President of the college, and his brother, Don Earl was one of his professors. The fact that I had been raised in the Minneapolis area, was one of the main reason I chose to attend Minnesota Bible College. Also, the Boatman brothers being there was a strong influence on me, as they were among the few Christians I knew at that time in my life. As I recall, I had twenty dollars, and two passengers, Mary Boatman and Eleanor Anderson. My two passengers agreed to help pay for the gas for the trip. There was not much room in that little coupe; however, in those days we were all very skinny, so we fit into the car quite easily. Someone got the idea of painting a slogan on each of the three cars that were going to Minnesota. Danny Burris had a 1937 Ford. Blacky Blackwell had a 1935 Ford. The two of them decided to lead the way with my 1936 Chevrolet bringing up the rear. They painted on Blacky's Ford, "Minnesota or Bust!" Danny's Ford followed with the words, "Minnesota or Drop Dead!" I followed with the words, "Me Too!" That is the name my coupe has affectionately taken for the past fifty or so years.

"Me Too" was a very special automobile. We have a photo of the coupe on the wall in our family room. Equipped with sixteen inch tires

*Jerry with Mrs. Schnaar while a student in San Bernardino Valley College*

my '36 coupe was one of the first cars with knee action that made it handle easy with an extra smooth ride. What I remember the most about "Me Too" is her very unique, but pleasant, smell that the mohair covered seats gave to her. It was that new car smell. It never left it. Also my coupe had a built-in Philco radio, which was very special at that time. The soft, dreamy music on that radio set the tone on the night I proposed to Normadeene at Loring Park in downtown Minneapolis. It was thirty degrees below zero. But the gas heater, frosted over windows, and soft Glen Miller music from the Philco made a perfect setting for the most important decision in my life, outside of my relationship to God, asking Normadeene Pletcher to be my wife, my life's helpmate.

## Chapter IX
## ON TO MINNESOTA BIBLE COLLEGE

We drove day and night, stopping only for gas. We could not afford to do otherwise. We drove on old Route 66. We drove over the then very treacherous Oatman Pass, which the two Fords had a very difficult time negotiating, and on into Oklahoma City. I noticed a motorcycle cop out of my rear view mirror. I also noticed that our caravan was traveling over the posted speed limit. I proceeded to slow down. People were looking at our three cars and laughing at the writing, "Minnesota or Bust!," "Minnesota or Drop Dead!," and "Me Too!" Old Route 66 went right through the center of the cities. There was no way you could escape the traffic. Then a strange thing happened. The motor cycle cop came along side of me and called out, "You better catch up with your buddies!" And to my surprise and delight, he escorted me up to the other cars.

Late that evening we pulled up in front of the Bridge Café, next to Minnesota Bible College and Levertan Hall, the girls dorm. I was out of gas. I had spent all of the twenty dollars I had when we started the trip. I walked across the street to the Bridge Café where I was met by Chris Capalis, the proprietor, who hired me on the spot to be a dish washer. Very few restaurants had automatic dish washers back then. I was about to begin a new phase in my life. "Me Too!" had safely brought me there, along with "my angel." You may be wondering how all of this has to do with angels? However, as I suggested earlier, as I look back, I am convinced now, more than ever, that it was my "unseen angel" that gripped the wheel of my 1929 Chevrolet coupe, and forced me over to the curb, and led me into that church that Sunday morning when I reached "the turning point" in my life.

Normadeene awakened one morning to tell me that she had been thinking of all that took place to bring me to her, and to Minnesota Bible College. She pointed out that I was a one-week-old Baby-in-Christ. I did not know very many Christians. I did not have any idea of what Bible College life would be like. I would once again be far away from my home and family. And I had little money to live on. I would be in a strange environment and culture. She suggested I was a classic example of the saying, "Fools rush in where angels fear to tread." However, what she didn't realize is that angels did not fear to tread with me.

# Chapter X
## A TEST OF INTELLIGENCE

Normadeene and I have often shared with our children, as well as those we have mentored through the years, the wisdom of the following statement: "A person's intelligence, is in direct proportion, to his or her ability, to adjust themselves, to the situation at hand." I was about to have a severe test of my intelligence.

Adjusting to Bible College life was not easy for me. I had enjoyed the freedom to make my own choices too long. Life in the Navy, and being a student on a secular campus made it very difficult for me to enter into the strict regimented life style demanded by the rules of ethics and conduct of Minnesota Bible College. I considered the code of morals and ethics that now confronted me far too confining for me. They were O.K. for narrow minded people, but not for one like me with my world view of life. I soon found myself in deep trouble with the Dean of Minnesota Bible College, the much feared Greek, G. H. Cachairas. I now have a large portrait of this beloved friend and fellow-laborer for Christ hanging over my desk.

I deliberately broke many of the rules of conduct set down by the Dean of Students. The rule that bothered me the most was that in regard to an evening curfew. We were supposed to be in our dormitories by 10 P.M. on weeknights, and midnight on weekends. I soon found a note in my mailbox telling me that the Dean wanted to see me. By that time, I had decided that Bible College life was not for me. I would take this opportunity to tell the Dean what I thought of his rules and regulations, in no uncertain terms, and head back for California. However, man proposes, but it is God who disposes, for when I entered Dean Cachairas' office, he greeted me with a warm and cordial smile and hand shake, and proceeded to tell me that he was in dire need of my help. He told me that many of the younger students were having a difficult time adjusting to campus life, and asked if I would help them to understand the reason for the many rules and regulations that they thought were foolish. This proved to be another turning point in my life, as I soon realized the reason for the discipline the Dean was attempting to instill in the lives of those future preachers and teachers and leaders in the Church of Jesus Christ.

Years later, after I had returned to Minnesota Bible College as a young professor, I inquired of Dean Cachairas, who by this time had become one of my dearest friends and mentor, as to why he did not expel me, as he had done with several other students, for even lesser offenses than I had been committing. He said, they knew better. They had been Christians for many years. He realized that I was a babe-in-Christ. He said that he and the rest of the faculty saw much potential in me, if I was given the time to mature. Both of us thanked God that his gamble with me proved to be the right one for both of us. Outside of the knowledge of the Bible I received in the next three years while attending Minnesota Bible College, as I suggested earlier, the most important thing that happened to me was meeting Normadeene Pletcher, a farm girl from Clarion, Iowa.

To begin with we were just good friends. I was dating her room mate, and she was dating my room mate. Somehow, we both broke off those relationships at the same time. I had such a deep desire to preach, that I had started preaching on Friday evenings at a little Open Bible Church in South Minneapolis. I had only been a Christian a couple of months and knew only one or two scriptures. The one that I used the most, and that I felt applied to me the most was I Timothy 1:15. "This is a faithful saying, and worthy of all acceptation, that Christ Jesus came into the world to save sinners, of whom I am chief." A.V. That described how I felt about myself very well, and served to get me started to fulfill the sense of urgency I felt in my heart to preach the Gospel. Thanks be to God, that after having preached for over half a century, that sense of urgency has never left my heart!

## Chapter XI
## A MARRIAGE MADE IN HEAVEN

One Friday morning, shortly after Normadeene and I had broken up with one another's room-mates, I asked her if she would lead songs for me at the Open Bible Church that night. She refused at first, but later called me to say she would accept the invitation. In the mean time, I had asked Marian Zimma from Redwood Falls, Minnesota, if she would lead songs that evening, to which she agreed. Thank God that His providence intervened, and I did not have the heart to tell Normadeene, so I decided to take them both with me that evening. Little did I

*Normadeene in her wedding dress*

*Normadeene and Jerry on wedding day*

know that this was the second most important decision I had ever made in my life. We squeezed into the little Chevrolet coupe, "Me Too," and drove to the church. I decided to have Normadeene lead singing, and I would sit with Marian. When Normadeene started to lead the singing, I knew immediately that she was going to be my wife. That was the first time I really saw her. It was a clear case of love at first sight! I saw the love of Christ radiating

*Wedding party at Normadeene's home on the farm with Me Too in the foreground*

out of her face. She had a very special gift, as she was able to sing as though it were a choir of angels. We took Marian home after the service, and then went back to downtown Minneapolis and spent the seventy-five cents I had in my pocket, and shared a fourth of a fried chicken and some toast to begin our new found relationship.

Normadeene bought a new set of tires for "Me Too" so we could drive down to Clarion, Iowa to meet her parents, on Valentine's Day week-end in February. The knee action on "Me Too" broke on the way down to Clarion, and cut off our brake lines. As the result, we did not get to Normadeene's home until 3 A.M. I will never forget the fear that came over me, seeing Normadeene's mother, Hattie Pletcher, standing in the front doorway, dressed in a long white nightgown, wearing a stocking cap, demanding an explanation for getting her daughter home at that wee hour in the morning!

*Jerry and his father-in-law*

We became engaged to be married on March 15th, and were married in Normadeene's home on the farm outside of Clarion, Iowa on Sunday afternoon June 13th, 1948. Normadeene's father, Bert Pletcher had suffered a heart attack, and was not yet fully recovered. He was one of he sweetest men I have ever known. He offered Normadeene the choice of having a large church wedding, or a small wedding at home, giving her the money it would have cost for a larger wedding. For several reasons, but mostly for the sake of her father's health, she chose the small home wedding. Her uncle Louis Aiken performed our wedding ceremony.

Once again, outside of accepting Jesus Christ as my Lord and Savior, Normadeene was, and still is, the single most important influence on my life. I am convinced that she was hand picked by God and His angels, just for me. From that time on, we have walked together where Angels dare.

## Chapter XII
## FILLING IN THE GAPS

Upon reflection, we believe it would be well to share several experiences we had while we were still students at Minnesota Bible College, as well as some interesting circumstances we faced while we were in Graduate School in Lincoln, Illinois.

As I suggested earlier, I had an insatiable desire to preach the Gospel. The first love that possesses one when he first finds the joy of salvation in his heart was burning in my bones, as was the case with Jeremiah. It is difficult for a novice, who had been a Christian for a little more than a year, to find a pulpit open to him. So I decided to do the next best thing, and that was to establish a place to preach for myself. I organized a group of students who were evangelistic minded to canvas a new sub-division north of Minneapolis called Circle Pines. Once again, it was case of "fools rush in, where angels fear to tread." Some of the people who shared in this venture have kept in touch with me through the years. One of them was long time friend, Howard Cowan. He and I have had many a chuckle over some of the things that happened. It was indeed a very valuable learning experience for all of us.

On one occasion, we came to a house that had no doors. We heard a voice coming from the back of the house, so we walked to the back. There was a man leaning out of a window asking what we wanted. We invited him to the services, and to this day, we wonder why there were no doors in that house.

We were encouraged by the interest many expressed in having church services in Circle Pines, so we contacted the local school board to see if we could rent their grade school building. They agreed to let us rent it for a very small fee. It was here that we met the custodian, Pa Lewis, whose wife became our very first member. They had a teen age daughter, Joan, who also proved to be a valuable asset, as she had many teen age girl friends who became active members in the youth group we established. We found that if we could reach the parents of the young people, it would not be long before we would reach them, also.

I well remember our first worship service. Pa Lewis had arranged the chairs and other furniture in a way that we could have preaching, teaching, a communion service, as well as fellowship. I had never been so nervous in my life, as I was that morning. I can still see the young two year old boy who raced back and forth in front of me while I was attempting to deliver the morning sermon, and the three year old girl who decided to partake of communion before the rest of us. The mothers of each never made a move to subdue their child. A well known evangelist from Austin, Minnesota came to conduct our first revival service. He was an excellent speaker, and moved the hearts of those who came to hear him. I had my first baptisms during those special services, nineteen in all. I recall that the baptistry had a sheet metal bottom. When you stepped on it, it made a thumping sound. A rather large lady, who desired to be baptized asked if I hit their heads on the bottom of the baptistry, after hearing that sound.

It was while we were preaching at Circle Pines that we had our first child, Albert Joseph. We named him after Normadeene's father who did not have a son. It pleased him beyond words. "Gibby," as we lovingly referred to him, could not have been named after a more wonderful man. Normadeene delivered "Gibby" in Hampton, Iowa's Community Hospital. I will never forget the joy of seeing our firstborn. We had dreams for him and his future. He hasn't disappointed us, as he has grown up to be a fine Christian man and an excellent minister of the Gospel. He is a loving and caring husband and father. We thank God for the blessing he and his family have been to our lives. His wife, Beth, and his two daughters, Emily and Anna, have also grown up to be fine, lovely young women.

I was very concerned over the fact that the small one room apartment in which were living, in the married couples side of Leverton Hall, did not have a sink, or any running water or plumbing of any kind. We shared a kitchen and bath with several other married couples. Our brother-in-law, Normadeene's sister Lois' husband was a plumber as well as a farmer. Concerned for our situation, he offered to travel to Minneapolis and install running water and a sink in our apartment. That would prove to be a tremendous help to us, bringing home a small baby. However, he made one stipulation. He had heard a father and son evangelistic team, Luke and Paul Raider, on the radio, and desired to hear them speak at their tabernacle on Lake Street in Minneapolis. I agreed to comply with his request. However, at the time, I had little knowledge as to the predicament that promise was to place the two of us in.

Jack completed the work of putting in a sink with running water earlier than expected. So as I had agreed, we headed for Luke and Paul Raider's Gospel Tabernacle. As we approached my car a young man who was rather strange, which is probably the understatement of all time, Dick Howitzer, came walking toward us. I proceeded to introduce him to Jack Rampelberg. Not knowing Dick, Jack invited him to go with us to hear the Raider's. He jumped at the opportunity. We were hoping to get there early so we could get seated in the back of the auditorium. Unfortunately we got there too late and were ushered by big, strong men to the front of the tabernacle. I mention that the ushers were big, strong men due to what was about to happen. Our ushers, along with the other ushers, took their places with the choir on the stage.

The man presiding over the services decided to take an offering. It was supposed to be a "free will" offering. At that time in my life, my resources were very skimpy, and I let the offering plate pass by without placing money in it. So did Jack and Dick. The presiding officer proceeded to express his disdain at those, he referred to as "cheapskates" who did not participate in the offering. He decided to have the offering plates passed a second time; however, with the same results from the "cheapskates." By this time I had already begun to feel rather uneasy over the situation I had gotten us into. Dick had positioned himself between Jack and myself.

Then it happened! Paul would proclaim and Luke would expound. Their theme for the evening was to prove that America is the true Israel, and the real "Promised Land," and even went so far as to say that George

Washington was actually Moses. As they spoke, our guest, Dick Howitzer, had worked himself into a frenzy over what he was hearing from the father and son team. He would first nudge me and then he would nudge Jack. We tried desperately to ignore him. We were hoping and praying that he was being ignored by others also. However, we soon found that was not the case. One of the speakers stopped abruptly and cried out, "You three jackasses there in the front row! You had better settle down or we will throw you out of this building." I did not believe it was actually happening. It was like I was having a night mare or an awfully bad dream. I thought what if my church heard about this, or the Bible College? Our tormentor went on to say that if he even saw a smile on our faces we would be thrown out bodily from the premises. I thought to myself, he need not worry about me. I was far too embarrassed to smile over our situation. Then, an awful thought came into my mind. What if I would smile, or even laugh a little? The more I thought about it, the more worried I became. Then, it happened. A chuckle found itself in the pit of my stomach. The more I thought about it, the bigger it got, and the more desperate I became. What was I to do? The chuckle wanted to come forth, like the urgency of a baby wanting to be born from its mother's womb. I decided to look over at Jack Rampelberg. Jack was an elder in the Clarion, Iowa Church of Christ. He was very serious minded. By now, I believed he must be very angry over the situation I had gotten him into. That was a near fatal mistake, for as I looked over at Jack, I noticed he had a big broad "chessicat" grin on his face. That's all it took. The pent up chuckle in the pit of my stomach came roaring forth. Jack joined me. In a matter of moments, the two of us found strong, powerful hands on us. They ripped off my tie, scratched my face, and proceeded to usher Jack and me out of the tabernacle. They never laid a hand on Dick Howitzer, however. The men were headed toward a large plate-glass window. They somehow changed directions and proceeded to throw us out onto the cement sidewalk, and closed the doors after us. I prayed that this incident would not get back to the members of my church in Circle Pines. I learned later that Paul Raider was a personal friend of Russell Boatman, the President of Minnesota Bible College. They played hand ball each week at the Athletic Club. Paul Raider expressed his anger to Russell Boatman over the men who had attempted and succeeded in disrupting the services at his tabernacle. I have often asked myself, "Where was my angel that night?" I am now convinced that he steered those big, strong men away from that plate-glass window and helped soften the fall as we hit the sidewalk outside the tabernacle. Jack and I have shared many a chuckle over that night at Luke and Paul Raider's Gospel Tabernacle through the years that have followed. We had many other very interesting experiences while ministering there. One of them stands out in my mind that I believe I should share at this time.

The husband and father of two of the people who were baptized during our revivals, who I will refer to as Jack Beck, was an inmate in Stillwater Penitentiary. I was asked to visit him. I had never made such a call before. Each time I had to present proof of being a minister of the Gospel. After several such meetings, he expressed his desire to receive Jesus into his heart and be baptized into Christ. I wanted to be sure that he was sincere, so grilled him as to his motive. He convinced me that he was ready to start a new life. On the way out of the prison that afternoon, I gained an audience with Warden, Mr. Utech to ask his permission to baptize this man. He agreed until I explained that we baptize by immersion. He proceeded to tell me that would not be possible, as there were not facilities in the prison where that could be done. I asked him if I could take him to a Baptist Church in Stillwater. He said that would not be possible. He further stated that only an action from the Governor of the state could make that possible. I then asked him if I could bring in a "portable baptistry." At the time I had never heard of such a thing myself. He flatly refused my request.

As I left him, I reminded him that many do not want to be baptized, but here is a man who desires to obey the Lord Jesus, and you will not allow it. You are responsible for this man's eternal soul! As I look back, I believe I may have been a bit too hard on him. However, the end in this case, did justify the means. Upon arriving home, I received a message from Warden Utech telling me that I was free to baptize Jack Beck in any way I could manage it. As I recall, Warden Utech had a big black cigar in his mouth when I was speaking to him. He kept moving it around and around in his mouth. I thought I was nervous, but he was even more nervous than I was.

That baptismal service at Stillwater Penitentiary was a beautiful sight to behold. I went to a tent and awning company and asked them to put clues in a piece of canvas that I could lash up with rope. A group of students, along with President Russell Boatman accompanied me to the prison. One of the students, Winton Zastrow, had a beautiful tenor voice. We were able to place our baptistry in a mop-tub in cell block number 17, and fill it with water. The Bible college students and President Boatman held it up as Jack Beck and I climbed into it. Winston Zastow sang the gospel song, "The Old Rugged Cross." The strains of his powerful voice echoed through the stone walls of that cell block. There was not a dry eye in that place, as the guards themselves stood there with tight throats and tears in their eyes. Jack Beck still had to pay his debt to society. He was not free, as the world calls free. However, he had the only real freedom, which comes from the truth that Jesus The Prince of Peace offers. John 8:32 This was the first baptism by immersion in that prison, and maybe so, in any American prison.

# Part III
# ME TOO

A True Story about Angels

## Chapter XIII
## AN ANGEL IN THE NIGHT

In my senior year of Bible college, I decided to re-enlist in the Active Reserves of the Naval Air Corp. This would later prove to have a profound affect on our future, and serve to enhance our faith in the reality of our Guardian Angel.

Danny Burrus and Blacky Blackwell joined me in the decision. We would report once a month to the Naval Air Station in Minneapolis on weekends. In this way we could maintain our longevity in the Navy, and also pick up a little extra pocket money. As suggested above, little did I realize the effect this decision could have on Normadeene's and my life and ministry. It was peace time—we felt secure. The war in Korea had not yet started, and we felt it was a relatively safe decision. I graduated from Minnesota Bible College in May of 1950. We accepted the call to become minister of the Youngstown Christian Church in Youngstown, Illinois. We had previously established the Circle Pines Christian Church North of Minneapolis, so had some experience ministering to a church. Before starting our duties with The Youngstown Christian Church, we traveled to California to visit my mother and father, as well as the rest of my brothers and sisters. My brother Harlow decided to come back with us to Youngstown and finish his senior year of high school with us. We were delighted to have him with us.

On the way back to Illinois, we stopped over in Clarion to visit

Normadeene's family, and while we were there I was to be ordained into
the ministry formally, at the Goldfield Church of Christ. Normadeene
had been baptized at that church several Years earlier. At that time, most of
my family were not members of a non-denominational Christian church,
and thought that I had become a fanatic. I think that they also thought I
was passing judgment on them. As I look back, I can understand why. In
my zeal to share my new found faith, I had not yet learned to start with
people where I found them, and not where I wanted them to be. I must
have been like a bull that carried it's China closet with him. However, I
simply wanted them to know that *God has no grandchildren.*

*Jerry's first congregation at Circle Pines*

I was asked to stop off on the way to Goldfield to answer some questions, one of my brother-in-law Jack Rampelberg's hired men had, in regard to the design and purpose of Christian baptism. I forgot that Harlow
was in the back seat of the car. When I pulled out of the drive way, I asked
Harlow, "Do you think I did him any good?" He replied, "I don't know

*Wayne Armstrong's daughter Rebecca on her wedding day with Benjamin*

about him, but you convinced me!" I had the privilege of baptizing Harlow, before I was ordained, that evening. Harlow was the first person to be baptized in the new church building where the church was meeting.

Youngstown was a very small farming community, and we soon found that we had far too much energy to confine ourselves to just that small community. While driving in the area one day, we came upon a little town, a few miles from Youngstown, called Greenbush. We soon learned that Abraham Lincoln had made Greenbush famous when he was a young lawyer, by participating in a trial there. We also observed a large white church building in the center of the town. Upon further inquiry, we found that it was a Methodist Church which had services once a month. They were conducted by the District Superintendent, Charles Wagner, who was sort of a circuit rider preacher. We asked the person who lived next door to the church if they might desire to have preaching every Sunday morning. We had noticed several young people, and thought there was a need for more frequent instruction in Christian living for those young people. We were asked how we, being with the Christian Church, could preach in a Methodist Church? We assured him that we would only preach from the Bible, and if ever we erred from that trust, they would simply have to ask us to leave, and we would comply. He said they would let us know.

Not long after, we began to drive over to Greenbush during the Bible school hour of the Youngstown Church. God had opened a wonderful door of opportunity for us.

Everything was going very smoothly, when the unthinkable happened and I received orders to return to active duty in the Naval Air Corp, as an Aviation Electronic Technician. It seemed that my experience was badly needed. The Navy had sent my orders along with a train ticket and meal ticket. What were we to do? My decision to join the Inactive Reserves during peace time had now come back to haunt me. The ministry at Youngstown was fruitful, and we were gaining a strong foothold in the Greenbush Methodist Church, as we were able to establish a very active youth group, which in turn had served to reach many of their parents who had not been active. We were called there, just to leave it all, when it seemed like God's strong hand had brought us to that ministry, at that time in our lives.

I decided to write a letter to the Commandant of the Ninth Naval Air District requesting for a temporary delay in my orders to return to active duty. I consulted with Russell Boatman, the President of Minnesota Bible College, asking him if he thought I had any recourse. He assured me that my situation was hopeless, and advised me to resign myself to going back into the Navy. The elders of the Youngstown Church wrote a letter stating the need for the church to have me as their minister, and suggesting that I would be more valuable to our country serving them as a minister of the Gospel, than returning to serve in the Navy. I was to leave on a Monday morning. We had received no reply from the Commandant of the Naval Air District. That Sunday before I was to leave was a glum one. We spent the day in prayer and much tears. Neither church wanted us to leave, but it seemed we had no choice in the matter.

We went to bed that Sunday evening feeling very restless and uncertain for our future in the ministry. Harlow would have to return to California to finish his high schooling there. And Normadeene would have to go back to Clarion, Iowa and live with her parents until I could send for her. By this time, our first child, Albert Joseph, was about a year old, which further complicated our situation. I had just managed to doze off, when Normadeene started to scream! I looked to the foot of the bed, and there stood a large man with a glowing white body, and I thought he must have come from the railroad tracks that were near our house, during our Sundays evening service, and had been hiding in our closet. I jumped out of bed believing I was in for a life or death struggle with that large shiny white figure of a man. Normadeene continued to scream uncontrollably! I found myself looking right into the face of the man. I started to close my arms around him, expecting a mighty struggle, but to my surprise, the shiny figure of a man just seemed to melt away from my grasp.

I will never forget that face. As I think back, It was actually a kind face. It was a face that did not seem to want to do us any harm.

I proceeded to shake Normadeene to get her calmed down. When she got back her composure, I asked her what she saw. She said she woke up because she felt somebody breathing in her face. She then described the very figure of the man that I had just attempted to subdue. We had never been so scared in our lives! We frantically searched everywhere, but to no avail. We could not find anybody hiding in our room.

The next morning, the morning I was to leave for the Navy, our door bell rang. It was Western Union with a telegram stating that I had received an indefinite deferment from active duty! We could continue with the ministry God had sent us to accomplish. We slept with the lights on in our bedroom for a long time. We thought we were having hallucinations. We consulted with our family doctor. He told us that because we both saw the same thing, it could not be our imagination. Then, G. H. Cachairas came on Spring Tour to speak at the Youngstown Church. We recounted our experience to him. He immediately told us that God had sent an angel to tell us that we could continue our ministry. He told us that I should have remained calm and talked to him. I explained how frightened we were. I also recalled that it was exactly mid-night when the man appeared in our bedroom. That is the time that things like that often happened in the Bible. We are now convinced that Dean Cachairas was right. God sent my angel, but this time it was Normadeene's angel, too. We have never been the same since that frightening, but wonderful experience. We were assured once again, that God's strong hand is upon us, and His angels are guarding over us. (Psalms 34:7)

# Chapter XIV
## MORE GAPS TO BE FILLED

We had much to learn in our first ministry out of college. Hindsight is always better than foresight, and looking back, we are convinced we brought many of the difficult situations we faced on ourselves. We don't believe we made many errors of heart, but we do believe we made errors in judgment. That was because our knowledge and experience was limited. If we had it to over again, we would probably make the same mistakes, as we acted on the knowledge and experience we had up to that time.

The weight of the hands of the elders, on the night I was ordained into the ministry, laid heavy upon my heart. I felt a tremendous responsibility to be faithful to the teachings of the Bible. I was to "reprove, rebuke and exhort." However, I probably didn't do it with the "all long suffering and doctrine" that concluded Paul's admonition to young Timothy. II Timothy 4:2 I had not yet learned the wisdom of starting with people where you find them, not where you want them to be. I had never been told that more can be accomplished in a short time when people are ready than in a long, long time when they are not ready. God was about to allow us to be placed in "the refiner's fire," and teach us some important lessons the hard way, by experience, which is a difficult, but often the best teacher. Our faith was about to be tested and tried. It has well been said, "A scientist has to *see* to believe, but a Christian has to *believe* to see." God helped us to see.

Shortly after arriving in Youngstown, we started to have phenomenal success through the preaching of the Gospel. We baptized several prominent people in the community. One of them was the former Treasurer of the State of Illinois. Many of them had never heard a sermon on the design and purpose of Christian baptism. This is also the case with many people today. Most of them had inherited their religion from their parents. As we suggested earlier, we pointed out to them that God has no grandchildren. We were very careful to not leave the impression that we were right and they were wrong. On the contrary, we pointed out that we can both be wrong, but the Bible is always right. Therefore, it would be

*Jerry and Normadeene with "Gibby" and Cindy in the Youngstown Christian Church next to where the angel appeared to them*

our only guide of faith and practice. The result of preaching the Gospel of Jesus Christ to sincere people, will always be people being baptized into Christ. Galatians 3:27.

An elderly lady, who we will refer to as Myrtle, was the teacher of the Adult Bible Class on Sunday mornings. She was a graduate of Moody Bible Institute, and well versed in the Scriptures. She was much loved by the members of The Youngstown Christian Church, where I was the new Senior Minister. For some reason or other, she refused to accept the Bible teaching in regard to Christian baptism, and openly took issue with what I was teaching and preaching in her class. She went so far as to speak out loud during the worship services, while I was preaching, to express her disapproval of my messages. This was something I had never experienced before, and something I did not expect from a gentle mannered old lady. When I spoke to her to let her know the Scriptural basis of my preaching, she would counter with, "That may be what it says, but that is not what it means." She claimed that whenever baptism was mentioned, it referred to "Spirit" baptism, not "water" baptism. She was causing division in the church body. So I called our elders together, and presented them with the problem that was facing us with Myrtle. I asked their advice. They said I should confront her with what the Christian Church believes and teaches in regard to our differences, and said she must not openly disagree with that teaching in her classes, and especially during the worship services. If she was not willing to do so, the elders suggested that she resign from teaching her class. In retrospect, I now believe the issue may have been handled in a more diplomatic and kinder way. After all, Myrtle had taught that class for many years. She had spent much time in study and preparation. We should have shown respect for her age, and appreciation for the time and energy she had put into teaching her class. Also, I believe now that it was the elder's responsibility to confront Myrtle, and not a young man fresh out of Bible College, who was hardly dry behind the ears, spiritually speaking, compared to her. And even though she was causing us much frustration, Normadeene and I loved her dearly. We did not want to lose her friendship or incur her wrath. However, in obedience to the elders, I confronted Myrtle with their decision. She chose to resign, and immediately got on the telephone and called all of her friends, and the members of her class, and told them that our new preacher, Jerry Gibson, kicked her out of her class. Little did I know what Normadeene and I were now in for. Nobody bothered to ask my side of the story. All they could think of was, that a mean spirited young preacher, had abused poor Myrtle. Nobody bothered to mention that it was the decision of the elders, not Jerry Gibson.

In a small community, nothing can be kept secret for any length of time. By the next morning, everybody knew how Myrtle had been mistreated by Jerry Gibson, and they were angry!

The General Store in Youngstown was the place where all of the men from this farming community would meet to gossip, discuss farm prices, and any other topic that was of interest to them. Our neighbor, who I will refer to as Calvy, was the owner and proprietor of that store. One could buy everything from milk and bread or nuts and bolts at his store. Calvy was a very enthusiastic, red head, who reminded me of a "Bantam Rooster." I walked into his store on Monday morning to buy a loaf of bread and a quart of milk. Up until that time, we were the best of friends.

I felt a cold, loud silence when I entered that store. Suddenly, Calvy came charging out from behind the counter shouting, "Is it wrong to kill an old lady? Is it wrong to kill an old lady?" I told him I did not know what he was talking about. He said he was referring to how I had mistreated Myrtle. He then, put up his fists and said, "Preacher, I want to fight you!" I was in total shock. My first impulse was to land a fist right on his jaw. However, it is no sin to be tempted. It is only a sin when one yields. I stepped back and informed Calvy that I was not going to fight him. He then began to call me a coward and ordered me out of his store. I tried to tell him that it was the decision of the elders of the church and not mine, but he would not listen.

That was just the beginning. We started to get death threats. At this time I was driving to Greenbush every Sunday morning to preach in the Greenbush Methodist Church. Word got out that some of the men of the community were going to waylay me and drown me in the river. Taking their threat seriously, the elders hired a young man to ride shotgun in my car to secure my safe travel to and from the Greenbush church. Our ministry in Youngstown had now become one big nightmare! I had to leave Normadeene and Gibby home alone, while I traveled to Lincoln for Graduate School. I hated to do that, as we had continued to receive death threats.

One evening, while I was away in Lincoln, the town drunk, who I will refer to as Dale, walked into our house unannounced, and informed Normadeene that it was not safe for her and Gibby to stay in that house any longer. Other similar incidents happened in the next few months.

*Jerry and Normadeene with "Gibby" and Cindy relaxing at Lake Story near Galesburg, Illinois*

However, the most heartbreaking thing of all, for us, was the fact that several of the elders, who had helped make the decision to ask Myrtle to no longer teach her class, decided to distance themselves from us and defected to our opposition.

Normadeene was pregnant with Cindy all through this terrible time. She had to be rushed to the hospital several times in order to save the baby, due to the strain she was under. Thanks be to God, Cindy was one of the bright spots in our ministry at Youngstown, as she was born a very beautiful, healthy baby in the St. Francis hospital at Macomb, Illinois. She has grown up to be an on-fire Christian, as well as a loving wife and mother.

While this was happening in Youngstown, our ministry in Greenbush was thriving. The time came when the elders of Greenbush asked me to come to Greenbush as their full time minister. The timing was perfect. It got us away from our miserable situation, and allowed us to give our full time to serving the Greenbush church.

Our angel was with us all through our trials in Youngstown. He protected us from the anger of those men in Youngstown. He rode beside us when we traveled from Youngstown to preach at Greenbush. I have often admonished that we should not insult God by rejecting His message or His messenger. It is interesting to note that every man who raised a hand or voice against us while we were in Youngstown seemed to incur the wrath of God. Calvy went broke and lost his business. One of the elders that forsook us went insane. Another lost his farm. Before we left Greenbush, every last one of them came to ask our forgiveness, which we freely gave.

We finished our work in Lincoln Christian College in the Spring of 1955. During my last year of graduate school, I took over some of the classes of one of the professors who resigned. It was valuable experience for me, as I was soon to become a professor at my old alma mater, Minnesota Bible College, but not without some interesting circumstances with another college.

During our last year with the Greenbush church, I held my first revival and helped start a new church in Beardstown, Illinois. I remember Elder P.B. Holland, who traveled to Greenbush to ask me to conduct those services. It was a very rewarding experience. We met in the Masonic Hall. We had over fifty people respond to the Gospel invitation. The church is now meeting in their own beautiful church building.

Our ministry at Greenbush was a happy and rewarding experience. One of the most wonderful experiences was the fact that during our last year, our youngest son, G.A., Gerald Jr. was born. He has grown up to be a fine young man who has brought much joy into the lives of the Gibson family. Our experience in Youngstown and Greenbush was a time of preparation for what was to come. The primitive conditions in which we lived, in Youngstown and Greenbush, were in some respects, more difficult than what we experienced in Africa. I can't emphasize enough how courageous a minister's wife must be, and how many difficult situations she subjects herself to when she marries a preacher. That is why I will point out, later in another book, the African people respected Normadeene so much they honored her with the title of "Mama." Subjecting herself and her children to the dangers and hardships of a strange African climate and culture, risking their very lives, expressed a love they had seldom experienced. Our house in Youngstown had running water and indoor plumbing. However,

*Jerry at the Greenbush Church*

the furnace was a coal furnace that required hand shoveling coal to keep it burning. That was heavy, dirty work for a young women. We did not have a refrigerator or washer and dryer. We had an icebox, that required twenty-five pound blocks of ice, to keep our food from spoiling, and P & G soap, a washtub, and scrub board, and a clothesline with clothespins to keep our clothes clean. We ate a lot of pork and beans, and every now and then, a farmer would bring us some fresh vegetables, eggs and meat. In fact, one of the farmers rented a meat locker for us and butchered a goat for us to eat. He had beef and pork in his own locker. When we moved to Greenbush, one of the farmers asked me if we liked beef or pork. I told him that we liked beef, but also liked pork. From time to time he would bring us some of both, for which we were very grateful. Our maximum, total combined salary, from both Youngstown and Greenbush, was forty dollars per week. Feeding three children and a wife, along with paying for a car and transportation to and from Lincoln, forced me to work part time as a carpenter's helper for John Springer, who paid me a dollar per hour for my labor. Mixing double batches of cement, by hand, and pouring it from the wheelbarrow into the forms, is what caused me to have back problems for many years to come. My ministerial tasks, along with attending graduate school and my part time job, left little time for much leisure activity. Living conditions in Greenbush truly tested Normadeene's faith and dedication. She could well have complained and become bitter over what she had to put up with. But she never did. We had no running water, not even a sink. We lived in a farmer's hired man house. Our toilet was an outhouse, in which the floor had rotted away. We became well acquainted with a Sears Roebuck and Montgomery Ward catalog, which we referred to as a wish book. During the winter months, the trek out to that house out back, was the coldest forty yards we have ever experienced. The men of the church promised that we would be provided with better living quarters in the future. I was away in graduate school, down in Lincoln, for most of the four years we lived in Greenbush. So Normadeene had to bare the brunt of this hardship all by herself, along with Gibby and Cindy. By the time G.A. was born we had moved to a house with a sink and running water, but still without an indoor toilet.

Those were long, lonely, cold and scary nights for Normadeene, home alone with our children. We did not have storm doors or windows on the hired man house, so they covered the doors and windows with a semitransparent sheet of plastic. The plastic material made strange noises when the wind whistled through it.

In order to obtain water, we had to climb over a barbed wire fence into a barn lot next to our house. There was a rusty handled old pump that was used to provide water for the cows that were pastured there. The cows would rub against the pump, and as a result, cow hair would fall into the water below. We had to pump several buckets of water in order to get a clean bucket of water. The word clean may be stretching the truth. However, we boiled the water before we drank it. We also did this when we were in Africa.

On one occasion, when I was away in Lincoln, Normadeene woke up to a strange scratching noise coming from one of the windows. She immediately thought that somebody was attempting to break into our house. She was all alone with the children, and she was terrified. She decided she had better look to see who it was. She looked, and there was an ugly face looking in at her. For a moment she thought that some kind of mad man was trying to get her. Then, she realized that what she saw was the face of a cow that was peering into her window. We were very glad to move to a house that was a little better to live in. From that time on, we were convinced that our living conditions would only get better. As suggested earlier, all of this was part of God's plan to prepare us for our future ministries. We are convinced that our angel was always there, watching over us, as God had promised, during our ministry in Youngstown and Greenbush.

I think it is important to mention, that none of the victories we enjoyed, or defeats we suffered, while in Lincoln Christian College's Graduate School, would have happened had it not been for my long time friend and room mate, Wayne Armstrong. He paid my first semester's tuition, without which, I could not have enrolled in Lincoln Christian College. The President of the college at that time was Earl Hargrove. He made a special visit to Wayne and myself to challenge us to take advantage of the new degree program they were adding to their curriculum. They were offering a Master of Theology Degree, as well as a Doctor of Theology. He reasoned with us that it was not fair for a minister to have to work seven years for a B.D. degree when a person in a secular school could receive a doctorate in seven years. We were more or less guinea pigs in the program, as we both accepted his challenge. As I suggested earlier, without the financial help of Wayne Armstrong, I could never have been able to enter into that program, at what was then known as Lincoln Christian Institute.

Both of us completed the residence requirements for both the Masters and Doctoral program. However, at the time we were completing the work for the Doctorate, the college decided to discontinue the Doctoral program.

Many things in a person's past, some small, and some of greater import, have a profound effect for the rest of our lives. That is why the preacher in the book of Ecclesiastes admonishes, "Remember your creator in the days of your youth." Eccl. 12:1. Why? So we don't do things when we are young that we will be sorry for all of the rest of our lives. You can pound a nail into a piece of wood, and when you pull it out it will leave a scar. This has always been our prayer for our children and grandchildren. However, it is also important to realize that the past is not to be lived in, but to be learned by. The years I spent in the Navy taught me a valuable lesson in discipline. In order to make my seven O'clock class in Lincoln, I had to leave at about 4:30 A.M. on Tuesdays. Because I attended school all year around, as we were allowed to take a limited number of hours of class work, I did this for more than four years. It was a little over 100 miles from our house to Lincoln, on roads that left much to be desired. During the winter months, the roads were often covered with snow and ice, that made for treacherous driving conditions. I am confident that my angel was with me as I traveled to and from Lincoln each week. The satisfaction was well worth the sacrifice. I taught the people I have mentored, starting with my own children, "if it doesn't cost anything, it isn't worth anything." The most valuable transaction ever made was Jesus Christ on the cross!

When we were in Africa, we made it a point to do nothing for the Africans that they could better do for themselves. We did the same with our children. We paid for their first year of college and they worked their way through the next three years. We seldom appreciate what we get for nothing. Today, they thank us for that, as it taught them valuable lessons in how to be responsible and accountable. Those two principles are what Noah Webster said were the most valuable lessons he had learned in life, that he was responsible and accountable for his own actions. God has given us the freedom to make choices, but He has not given us the freedom to choose the consequences of those choices. We indeed reap what we sow. Gal. 6:7. My five years in Lincoln were full of many rewarding, and sometimes humorous experiences. Wayne and I arrived in Lincoln needing a place to room for two nights a week, Tuesday and Wednesday nights. After several weeks of temporary housing, we were able to find a permanent place to hang our hats at the home of Mr. & Mrs. Fred Hild. We stayed with them throughout the remainder of our days in Lincoln, and became a part of their family, as they made us feel loved and cared for, like any other member of their family. Tragedy struck them when their son returned home from military service, only to drown in a near by gravel pit. I don't think they ever fully recovered from that crisis in their lives. However, the words of the Psalmist, "Weeping may endure at night, but joy comes in the morning." Psalms 30:5, and I Thessalonians 4:13, did bring much comfort to their hearts. Wayne and I shared a double bed, and in the same room, Eugene Hetzel and Glen Hull also shared a bed. The four of us had many an interesting theological discussion into the late hours of the night during those months we shared a room at the Fred Hilds. One afternoon, when Wayne and I needed a break from the rigors of the class room, we decided to drive into Springfield, which was some thirty miles away, and take in a movie. It was late when we got started, so we arrived home after midnight. We both had seven o'clock classes in the morning, so were both very tired. By the time we reached our one-o'clock class in the afternoon with Professor Bob Drake, we could hardly keep our eyes open. It was a seminar class on the subject of epistemology (theories of knowledge). Even though Professor Drake had an excellent grasp of the subject, his presentation was dry and boring. Especially so, at that time of day. He proceeded to explain to the class, which included Wayne and myself and also James Straus and Roger Elliot, how that often time different people view the same thing in a different light. He used the example of a color blind person who approaches a red stop light, but thinks it is a green light. By this time, Wayne Armstrong lost the battle to stay awake. It was very warm in the class room, which added to his dilemma. He started to lean over on me. I attempted to straighten him out, and pushed him away. By that time, his eyes were closed and his mouth was wide open. He continued to fall over on me. Professor Drake continued to explain how the woman saw a red light but thought it was a green light. Suddenly, he stopped and demanded of Wayne, "What did she think she saw?" Wayne looked up and mumbled, "She thought she saw a puddy cat." Professor Drake was stunned by that reply. Slowly he started to laugh, and continued until all of us in that class room were rolling on the floor with uncontrollable laughter. To this very day, we still get a hearty chuckle out of recounting that experience. Needless to say, Professor Drake dismissed the class early that afternoon.

As suggested, we owe a great debt to Wayne and to Lincoln Christian College, also, because those five years helped prepare us for our many years in Christian education, and were another major cross-road in our lives. I might also add, that we have had an excellent relationship with the college through the years, in spite of the disappointing experience with my degree. I was invited back often to speak in their chapel while I was a Campus Minister for the University of Illinois, and during Leon Appel's tenor, as President of the college, I was invited to be the speaker for two Spiritual Emphasis Weeks, and one of them was extended for a second week, due to the spiritual awakening that took place on the campus. I treasure a picture I have with my son Albert Joseph, and a group of students praying at the front of the chapel with Leon Appel's arms around my neck. These are the memories I hold dear of Lincoln Christian College and Seminary. How I thank God for the faithful, true to the Bible, teaching and preaching that has gone forth from her halls through the years, and the multitude of preachers and teachers of the Gospel of Jesus Christ, as well as other specialized Christian servants, who have carried the Christian message to the very ends of the earth. I take great joy, as well as grateful pride, in the words of her first President, Earl Hargrove, "Here come the preachers!" If it had not been for his challenge to Wayne Armstrong and myself, who knows how different our lives, and the lives of countless others, might be today.

One more interesting side note to my friendship with Wayne Armstrong. Wayne spent many years as a professor at Lincoln Christian College. Normadeene was a very close friend of his first wife, Shirley, who died at an early age, childless, except for their adopted son, Phil. However, he was blessed with a wonderful second wife, Barbara, who was the school nurse. Their marriage was blessed with three beautiful daughters. I had the privilege of officiating at the wedding of their daughter, Rebecca, who married Benjamin Li Liang, who we met while we were lecturing in Beijing, China. I had the opportunity to present the Gospel to the scholars of The Institute for Research of World Religions. He came to me by night to tell me that his heart burned within him while I was sharing the Gospel message. He said he was very lonely when we first began to talk. Before he left, he confessed his faith in Jesus as the Son of God and his savior. He said he was not lonely any more. I will have much more to say about this at a later time. I want to give special honor to the Greenview Christian Church in Centralia, Illinois, and their precious departed preacher, Howard Newlin and his wife Anita, for the part they have played in Benjamin and Rebecca's lives, as they made possible his attending both Lincoln Christian Seminary and Trinity College. While attending Lincoln Christian Seminary, he met Rebecca. Little did Wayne ever imagine, that his old class mate, Jerry Gibson, would travel to China and bring back a husband for one of his daughters. It is indeed a true saying that, "Man proposes, but it is God who disposes."

## Chapter XV
## PRESIDENT FOR A DAY

It has well been said, that a teacher imparts far more than academic knowledge to his students. He also, imparts personality. As I think of the influence the various professors I sat under had on me, both at Minnesota Bible College and Lincoln Christians Seminary, I can agree with that evaluation.

At Lincoln Christian Seminary, Raymond Phillips, Winfield Richards, S. Edward Tesh, Enos Dowling, Marian Henderson, Harold Ford, Robert Drake, and of course, Earl Hargrove, all had a tremendous influence on my future ministries.

At Minnesota Bible College, Don Earl Boatman, Conley Sylsby, William Homer Sperry, Russell Boatman, Lawrence Sunkler and Ronald Keeler, also, had a profound influence on my immediate and future life. However, the two men who influenced my life and my thinking the most were Dean G. H. Cachairas and Professor Monson E. Miller. Dean Cachairas lit a fire in the bones of all the young men whose lives he touched. His class room was always like a revival meeting. We would break out in the middle of his class and sing "Revive us Again"! Dean Cachairas had a tremendous love for lost souls! He also set an example of commitment and faithfulness to the Word of God like very few men I have known. When he spoke, it was always with authority, backed up with a "thus saith the Lord," as only the Greek scholar he was could do. He always gave one a

Scriptural answer to a question pertaining to the faith and practice of the church. The time I spent sitting under his feet as a student, and the time I later spent as his colleague on the staff of Minnesota Bible College, is time I will forever cherish. He indeed had a tremendous influence on my life, as well as all those who had the privilege of knowing him. He indeed imparted part of his personality to me. I have had people tell me that I sound like Dean Cachairas when I speak. I have a large portrait of the beloved Dean hanging on the wall above my desk. Professor Miller, on the other hand, had an entirely different personality than Dean Cachairas. However, they were very close friends with mutual respect for one another. Professor Miller was much more laid back than Dean Cachairas. He was a very wise Patriarch type of person who always had time to listen. Like Jesus, he was never in a hurry. It was easy to get him off of the subject in the class room, because there was no question a student could ask that Professor Miller felt was not worthy of an answer. He was a caring man who demonstrated the principle, start with people where you find them, not where you want them to be. He always had time for you. His office was open after hours, even on Monday morning when he had returned from preaching at Fillbrook, late Sunday night. He was there to listen to the concerns and heart aches of the young student preachers who had returned from their week-end ministries. I recall one such occasion vividly. I had worked all week long, with every spare moment I had from my class room work, to prepare a sermon for Sunday morning at Circle Pines. I still remember the title of that sermon. "All Beginners are Children." It was from the first chapter of Jeremiah, where Jeremiah protested, "I can not speak for I am but a child." I had never worked harder on a sermon, and was anxious that I get my message across that morning. It seemed to fall on deaf ears. Perhaps I tried too hard. I was devastated. The first thing on Monday morning, I knocked on Professor Miller's office door. He graciously ushered me into his office and asked in a rather drawl like tone of voice, speaking very slowly, "Brother Gibson, what can I do for you?" I told him of my experience on Sunday with the Circle Pines Congregation. He listened sympathetically. I then asked him, "If I preach a sermon on Sunday morning, how long should I wait until I preach it again?" I was determined to get that message across. Professor Miller sat back in his chair, and with his slow drawl like manner, replied, "If you preach a ser-

mon on Sunday morning, don't preach it again until Sunday night." I
preached the same sermon two weeks later, and it was the best sermon
they had ever heard. Professor Miller's advice was good.

I gave special attention to Professor Miller, because in the Spring of
1955, well into his eighties, he decided to retire from being Professor of
Old Testament and Practical Ministries. He would be hard to replace. In
fact, it would be impossible to replace him. Someone could take over his
classes, but it just would not be the same. I was completing my graduate
school education at Lincoln that Spring. I majored in New Testament for
my Masters Degree, and in Old Testament and Hebrew for my Doctors
Degree. President Boatman contacted me and asked me to send a résumé
to the Chairman of the Board of Trustees of Minnesota Bible College and
request to be a candidate for the vacancy in Minnesota Bible College's Old
Testament Department. It seemed that the timing was just right. This was
the first time that position had been open for many years. I had some
grave doubts about my qualifications for such a position. They were offering a full professorship to the candidate they would call. I was just twenty-
nine years old, and had only been a Christian for less than eight years. I
later found out that a very well qualified man, Ruben Ratzeloff, had already sent in his résumé. Ruben was at least ten years my senior at that
time.

Due to my long time friendship with President Boatman, I sent a
résumé to the Chairman of the Board of Trustees and waited for a reply.
Not long after, I received a phone call from President Boatman, followed
by a letter, telling me that all other candidates for the position had been
eliminated, and all that was left for us to do was to work out a contract
that would meet our mutual approval. Normadeene and I were elated!
This was indeed a dream come true. Think of it? Going back to Minnesota where I spent most of my youth, and to the Bible College where I met
Normadeene and received my first years of Christian education, and also
where the Golden Gophers played football. I was an avid fan for them
during my high school years. We said to ourselves, "This is too good to be
true!" Then it happened. I received a call from the acting President of
Platte Valley Bible College, Dr. Ellis Baker, in Scotts Bluff, Nebraska, asking me if I would consider becoming President of that Medical Missionary College. He did not ask me if I was interested in the position. He

asked me if I would consider it. That caused our dilemma. A very close friend of ours, Elwood Beeman, who was a class mate of mine, both at Minnesota Bible College and Lincoln Christian College, had great interest in the welfare of Platte Bible College. He recommended me to the Trustees of Platte Valley Bible College. I had absolutely no interest in becoming the C.E.O. of a Bible college that was way out in the west, where we thought civilization must be very primitive. It seemed like being called to a foreign land at the time. We thought of every reason possible for not accepting this call. However, Dr. Baker was very persuasive and would not take No for an answer. He finally persuaded us to drive out to Scottsbluff and meet with the Board of Trustees and at least look over the situation. We knew it would disappoint Russell Boatman, but we told him that we felt that if God wanted us to go to Platte Valley Bible College, rather than Minnesota Bible College, He would let us know. But it would take a trip to Scottsbluff, Nebraska to determine what His will was for our lives. Our reasoning was, not what we wanted to do, but what God wants us to do. That has always been a guiding principle in our lives. Russell Boatman told us that if we felt that way, we should travel to Scottsbluff. But he also secured our promise that we would make no announcement until after we had informed him. He was ready to make an announcement about our coming to Minnesota Bible College. Now, he would have to hold off such an announcement.

As I look back, I wonder how we ever made it to and from the places we had to travel. We have always prayed, the first thing, when we got into our cars, that God would surround our vehicle with angels. He has indeed answered that prayer, as we have been in situations where we lost control, and somehow have always escaped safe and sound. The trip to Scottsbluff was many miles away. We drove an old Studebaker Champion that was worn out when we bought it. It used a quart of oil every one hundred miles. The tires were bald and the brakes were suspect. We could not afford to stay in a hotel or motel, so we drove straight through. Because of the roads we had to travel in 1955 to get there, it took a full twenty-four hours. Upon arriving in Scottsbluff, we went directly to the Bible College. There we were greeted by a very warm and gracious Dr. Ellis Baker. He informed us we would be guests in his home. He said his wife Opal was anxious to meet us, so we left immediately for his place just west of

*Normadeene and Jerry with "Gibby," Cindy and G.A. just before traveling to Platte Bible College*

Scottsbluff, as I now recall. Opal also greeted us in a warm and friendly manner. She made us feel at home immediately. Their house, as I recall was a beautiful white colonial style house. One of the things we discussed was the desirability of living in the Scottsbluff area. The subject of tornadoes came up. He assured us that tornadoes seldom were seen in that area. Those were his famous last words in that regard, for before we left Scottsbluff to travel back to Illinois, a devastating tornado tore through Scottsbluff and the surrounding area doing thousands of dollars of damage. Normadeene and I saw it coming along the Platte River. It seemed to be chasing us. At one point we got of our car and laid flat in a ditch as it passed over us. We were approaching Dr. Baker's home and looked up, and there it was in his barn lot. It was then that we escaped to the ditch. Needless to say, Dr. Baker didn't have much to say about tornadoes after that. We met with the Trustees and faculty and staff of the college in several well planned meetings. They covered all of the bases, and somehow managed to convince us that Platte Valley Bible College was where God wanted us to be. They wanted someone with a preacher image as well as one who had the academic qualifications to gain the respect of the community. We could not think of a single valid excuse for not accepting the challenge, accept our own, selfish, personal desire to go to Minnesota Bible College. In a last ditch effort to get them to consider somebody else, I demanded of them a salary and other conditions of which I thought they would not be willing to comply. I went so far as to ask them to hire two professors of my choosing, Bill Griffin, who was a great source of encouragement to us during our difficult time at Youngstown, to teach New Testament and Greek, and Eugene Hetzel to teach the Old Testament. To our dismay, they willingly accepted all that we asked. That was our "fleece," so we were sure God wanted us there. I remembered our promise to Russell Boatman to not make any announcement until we first contacted him. So I obtained the promise from Dr. Baker and others to not make any announcements until after I had informed Russell Boatman. I told them I would call and let them know when they were free to publish our coming to be the new President of Platte Bible College.

We left Scottsbluff and traveled back to Illinois with mixed emotions and some apprehension. We would be the chief fund raiser and student recruiter for this fledgling new college. What we were going to do is what most missionaries have to do. *Go where they have not been, to do what they have not done, with money they do not have.*

The first thing I did, upon arriving back in Greenbush, was to sit down and draft a letter to Russell Boatman and let him know of our acceptance of the call to be President of Platte Valley Bible College. I dreaded writing that letter, but felt we owed it to him to let him know of our decision as soon as possible, so he could pursue another candidate for the position. While I was on the typewriter, our telephone rang. It was a very disgruntled Russell Boatman calling from Pine Haven Christian Service Camp in Park Rapids, Minnesota. He started by saying, "I am very disappointed in you, Jerry!" To which I replied, "Why, what have I done?" He said, "You promised not to make an announcement about your decision without first informing me!" To which I replied, "I know that, and I have not made an announcement." He then informed me that Dean Entrikin, from the Scottsbluff area, had walked into his cabin carrying a newspaper from Scottsbluff, with my picture on the front page, and the large caption, "New Administrator of Platte Valley Bible College." I had never been so embarrassed and disappointed in my life. I had given them a picture before we left, but had received their promise not to print anything until they heard from me. Somehow, there was a tremendous breakdown in communication. That was not the way to start out a working relationship. I failed to mention that Dr. Ellis Baker's brother, Paul Baker was also actively involved in the ministry of Platte Valley College. I have never known men of finer caliber, or with more integrity, than those two brothers. I am confident that there was no way that they would knowingly breach their trust with me. Nevertheless, I found myself in a very difficult situation. I apologized as best I could to Russell Boatman. I told him of the commitment I had secured from the powers to be at Platte Valley Bible College, and then assured him, that if Minnesota Bible College still wanted us, we would be there in time for the Faculty-Administration Retreat that was to be held before the Fall semester. I then called Dr. Ellis Baker and informed him as to what had happened. He apologized for the misunderstanding, and graciously accepted our decision to go to Minnesota Bible College.

We were willing to give up that which we could not keep, in exchange for what we can not lose. We would be called upon to do the same many times in the future. This was probably one of the most important junctures in our lives. Had we gone to Platte Valley Bible College, most of what follows would never have happened. Abraham was willing to give Isaac up to God, knowing the He who was able to bring to life the dead womb of Sarah, could also bring back his child of promise. God rewarded his faith by staying his hand, and providing a way out. God rewarded our faith, and through a series of circumstances, made it possible for us to do what we wanted to do in the first place. However, I will always remember that I was President of Platte Valley Bible College for at least a day. Once again, our angel was watching over us, as we saw how man proposes, but God disposes.

*Chapter XVI*
## THE MONEY-MAKING GARAGE

With the help of Jack Ramelberg, and several men from the Greenbush church, we moved from Greenbush, back to Minneapolis. We moved to an upstairs apartment, across from Van Cleave Park, in South East Minneapolis. It was like a breath of fresh air compared to where we lived in Youngstown and Greenbush. A concert pianist occupied the down stairs. We had to attempt to be very quiet, as she was annoyed by any noise we might make. It was early September, and we could already feel the cool breezes of Fall that help to make Minnesota such a beautiful place in which to live. There was a particular fragrance in the air that permeated the neighborhood where we lived. We lived by Van Cleave Park for a couple of months, and then moved to Kimble Hall, about five blocks closer to the college, so we could walk to school if necessary. We enrolled Gibby in first grade at a school close by. He was well received and did well as a first grader. We still remember the feeling we had in our stomachs that first day we sent him off to school. I also remember the first time he came home with his knees skinned, from a fall he had taken, and how Normadeene comforted him and applied soothing ointment to his wound. That was not the first or last time that scene repeated itself.

After a month or so, the saying, "God takes care of fools and Jerry and Normadeene Gibson" was truly demonstrated. A friend of Russell Boatman, Fred Kimble, who owned the apartment we were living in, approached me with an offer to buy one of his houses. Fred was terminally ill, and wanted to relieve his wife of some of the responsibility she would have to face after he was gone. The offer he made to us was almost unbelievable! He had a three story house at 1118 Seventh Street, within walking distance of the college. At that time, it was known as Kimble Attic, as the second floor, as well as the attic were both occupied by Bible College students and other women. It was in fairly good condition, but needed to be painted, a job that I could do myself during the summer months when school was out. It also had a four-car heated garage. In Minnesota, where it often warms up to twenty below zero during the winter months, that was a special treasure in itself. He offered to sell the house to us for no

down payment, no interest or carrying charges, for twenty thousand dollars, at one hundred dollars a month. We jumped at his generous offer. We became wealthy land lords. Rent from the upper two stories more than paid our monthly payments. We also fixed up a couple of married couples apartments in our basement. Our long time friends, Jack and Peggy Howard lived there after they were married. Several of the Anderson girls from Forest Lake, lived in the upstairs apartments. The house then became known as Gibson's

*Jerry after receiving his Master of Theology degree from Lincoln Bible Institute, with Normadeene*

Garret. Our heated garages were just an extra serendipity. We had people lined up to rent them whenever they became vacant. God's angels were surely watching over us.

One afternoon, I looked out of the window and saw that my garages were on fire. I called the Fire Department, and rushed out to the back yard to see if I could salvage anything. I have often quipped, "If you can keep your composure, when all around you are losing theirs, chances are, you don't understand the situation." As I stood there waiting for the firemen to get there, I felt a tugging at my trouser leg. I looked down, and there was Bobby Hoizington, the four year old son of my neighbor, who was the track coach for Central High School. I nervously inquired, "Bobby, what do you want?" He looked up at me and said, "Mr. Gibson, remain calm, remain calm." You see, he did not understand the situation. My money-making garage was on fire. I failed to mention earlier, that our salary as a full professor was two hundred fifty dollars per month, or a whopping three thousand dollars per year. So you see that the income from the garage was very important for us to meet our financial needs.

I mentioned Jack and Petty Howard, who moved into our basement apartment soon after their honeymoon, but I believe I should say more about them, as they have had a tremendous influence on our ministries through the years. I first met Jack when he came to MBC from Lebanon, Ohio, as a young Bible college student. He had worked for a year out of high school for National Cash Register in Cincinnati, Ohio. But then, through the preaching of his preacher, who I believe was Joe Randall, he committed himself to specialized Christian service.

I was on the top rung of a forty-foot extension ladder, standing on my tiptoes, painting the gable of our house. I realize just how dangerous that was, and how foolish I was to take that kind of risk. There was nothing, but my angel, to keep me from falling forty feet to the cement sidewalk below. Somehow, when you are young, you think you are indestructible. I know better now. Jack introduced himself to me, and we became fast friends. His wife, Peggy Snelle Howard, later became my secretary while I was a campus minister at the University of Illinois, and Jack was the Chairman of our ministry's board. He was also on the Board of Trustees of Mid-South Christian College. His parents were custodians and dorm parents there.

My years of teaching at Minnesota Bible College were a very wonderful and rewarding experience, which helped to prepare me for my other ministries through the years. To be more specific, it prepared me for ministries in Africa, as a missionary educator, on the university campus, as a teacher of religious studies, at Mid-South Christian, as a Bible College President, and especially for our ministry today with World-Wide Missions Outreach, headquartered in Lafayette, Colorado. I have often said, that in direct proportion to how we prepare ourselves, God will open avenues of service for us. We are now using every past ministry's experience to help us mentor the men and women we work with at The University of Colorado, and the university community as a whole. The most rewarding part of being a professor at Minnesota Bible College for thirteen years was the influence we had on our students. We had no clue just how much influence we had on many a life. I use the pronoun, "we," because Normadeene made a great impact on the lives of our students, out of the class room. She has the gift of loving hospitality, and her home and table were always open to them. Many of my students went on to make their mark in the Christian world. Russell Boatman's son, Charles became a Bible College President and had several other very successful ministries. Paul Carrier, Curt and Don Lloyd and Bob Cash, also became Bible College Presidents. Ronald Rife, who came from the Hessville Church, as did Paul Carrier, was Academic Dean at Dallas Christian College and is now working with his wife Doris, in their second tour of duty with Ghana Christian College. Others, such as Don Mechem, Leroy Randall, Sandy and Charlotte Sinclair, and many others were missionaries to foreign lands.

Bill and Dorothy Miller have served as professors and teachers at Nebraska Christian College for many years. Koula Beth Hazel and her husband Don are now working with prison ministries in Oklahoma. They are having a very fruitful ministry. Wally and Judy Robinson have worked with the military, where Wally was a Chaplain. Others became educators in secular institution, such as Bob Mignault, who also, has remained active in Wisconsin's Evangelistic efforts, as well as many other areas of Christian service. Bob Eckman and his wife Arlene have worked for years as counselors and educators in Montrose, Colorado, but have also been a powerful Christian influence in their community. Rodger McWaters, who attended both Minnesota Bible College and the University of Minnesota,

*Minnesota Bible College in background*

has made an impact in the secular world by his Christian influence. Others, such as Bill and Janet Smith, who are now ministering to The Cumberland Christian Church in Cumberland, Indiana, have actively supported our ministries financially through the years. We have had the privilege of speaking often in the churches they have served for revivals and other special services, such as Faith Promise Missionary Rallies. This is also true in regard to many of our former students. I will just mention a few others, who were students of mine, who have remained faithful in God's service throughout the years. Glen and Linda Anderson, Jerry Salsma, Gerald Albert, Mr. & Mrs. David O'Grady, Margaret Brownell, Darlene Scogin, who has been a Christian influence on the political scene. Jim and Carolyn Banta, Boyd and Bonnie Kuester, Bob and Judie Landry, Ralph and Esther Christman. Doug and Karen Wilson. There are many others of whom I will make mention at a later time. All of these have influenced our lives as much as we influenced them in ways they will never know.

As teachers, we often wonder if our students are listening to what we are saying. One of my main goals was to teach my students to think, and to think for themselves. I have often said, "Make people think they think, and they will love you. Make them think, and they will hate you." People do not want to think! It takes too much mental effort. Part of the reason Jesus was crucified was because he made people think. Often times, mental exercise is more strenuous than physical exercise.

One of my students, Ray August, came to Minnesota Bible College with a tremendous hunger for the truth. Due to his religious background, he had a very difficult time with many of the new truths, as far as he was concerned, that I presented in my class room. I made it a point to urge the class to think for themselves, and encouraged them to voice any questions they had with the material I presented. I told them they were welcome to disagree with me, but not to be disagreeable, or for difference sake. They had to have a logical reason for their ideas. But I was quick to point out that the more logical a theory may seem to be, the more erroneous it may be, if it is based on a faulty major premise. Many people confuse the role of one's conscience and intellect. The intellect informs, the conscience accuses. Yes, the conscience is not an informer. It is an accuser. Therefore,

*Gibson Garret where the money making garage caught on fire*

if our thinking is wrong, our feelings or conscience will also be in error. This is one of the reasons it is good to remember that we are not saved by our feelings, but by God's grace through faith. It is Ephesians 2:8&9, and Romans 10:17 kind of grace and faith we are talking about. I became very close friends with Ray and his fine Christian mother. I don't believe he was married to Marlene yet. Many years went by and, as is often the case, we lost contact with each other. Then after about forty years, Ray contacted me. Not long after, I received an envelope from Ray with a gift for our mission and a copy of the book he had published, *Time for Spiritual Tune-Up*. In the flyleaf, he made a note for me. He said I should turn to *x* in the preface. He had underlined a portion for me to read. The underlined portion reads as follows:

> A good friend of mine, Professor Jerry Gibson (See footnote at end of preface), some years ago talked about true wisdom and scholarship that made an indelible impression on me *that has influenced my life*. He taught that true scholarship not only requires, but demands honesty. An honest person will examine the evidence objectively in spite of their own preconceived ideas and beliefs and if the evidence substantiates it, they will change their position to line up with the truth. If it is true, it will line up with the Word for the Word is truth.
>
> I've had to re-evaluate some of my beliefs based on this study and have tried to follow this concept throughout this presentation.

Words cannot express the joy that came into my heart, knowing that in a small way, my teaching influenced a man whose book is now being read and studied by many. I have presented a copy of his book to the graduates from the University of Colorado, we are mentoring, as well as to the elders of the Christian Church of Broomfield where we are active members. As I suggested earlier, these are just a few, as there are countless other scholars I've taught in the college classroom, who have made a tremendous impact for the cause of Christ all over the world.

My classroom work demanded much from me. I worked hard on my preparation for each class. I taught Old Testament, Hebrew and Evangelism throughout my years there. I also taught Archaeology and Church History for a time. However, in spite of my demanding teaching load, I still had the energy to attend Post-graduate classes at the University of Minnesota which was right across from the Bible College. My classroom overlooked University Avenue and the University campus. Professor Howard Hayes joined me in this effort. We had many very interesting experiences while attending those classes. One of the classes we attended was "The History of Ancient Civilization" under Dr. Tom Jones. Dr. Jones wrote the text book for his class. Dr. Jones demanded a term paper, much reading, and a midterm and final exam for grading his students. The exams counted for half of our grade. He expected his students to be able to give back, almost verbatim, the things he had said in his lectures. He spoke very rapidly, and never looked a student in the eye, but stared at a spot on the wall in back of he classroom. I took meticulous notes, but due to Dr. Jones rapid speech, nobody could read my notes but me. I should have typed them out, but due to my very busy schedule, could not find the time to do so. A man from Indonesia was also in that class. He needed to score at least a B in that class to be able to continue his education in America. His name was Charlie. When it came time for our mid-term exam, Charlie approached me and asked if he could use my notes to study for the exam. He did not realize what he was asking of me? To comply, I would have to spend all night long typing my notes so he could read them. I had compassion on him, and agreed to do so. It also served as a good method of review for me. Charlie thanked me, and went on to achieve a B on the exam. One evening, Charlie approached me and said that I was different from the other people he had met. He went on to tell me he was a Muslim and was not satisfied with what the Muslim religion offers after death. He then asked me if I would meet with him and share what Christianity offers. I made an appointment for him to meet me in my office at the college. I went through the Gospel with him. He listened intently and seemed to comprehend what I was teaching. When I finished sharing the Gospel with him, he said, "That sounds too good to be true!" He went on to say that he had a very difficult time understanding how Jesus could be raised from the dead. His misunderstanding of what the Koran teaches was part of the reason for this. I shared with him Psalms 16:9,10, which is a wonderful prophecy of Jesus' resurrection from the dead. I also told him of Josephus, a great Hebrew historian's statement, "There was a man, if you can call him a man, Jesus Christ. He was crucified, but *three days later he rose from the dead.*" He stated this as a matter of fact. I prayed with him and did not speak with him for several weeks. It was during one of Dr. Jones' lectures, when he was talking about Socrates being accused of corrupting the Athenian youth and other crimes, during the first attempt at democracy in history. It actually failed because democracy demands an educated populace and that was not the case with Greece. He went on to tell how Socrates was urged by his friends to go into exile, rather than drink the hemlock cup which was an alternative. They pled with him, but he insisted that he would gain more by drinking the hemlock cup, than going into exile. He went on, in an attempt to comfort them, by saying death was not so bad, and perhaps there may be life after death. He had heard from a Jewish merchant of that possibility. I felt a nudging at my side. It was Charlie. He was holding up a sign he had made while Dr. Jones was speaking. It said, "Not death conquered Jesus, but Jesus conquered death!" Charlie became a Christian and went back to Indonesia and helped lead many others to Christ. Charlie was the first of many international students we have worked with. This eventually led to our establishing a campus ministry on the campus of the University of Minnesota. We later found out from Doug Dickey that our campus ministry at the University of Minnesota was the first in our brotherhood.

## Chapter XVII
## MINNESOTA BIBLE COLLEGE'S
## FACULTY AND STAFF

The men and women we were called to work with at Minnesota Bible College represented a vast amount of knowledge and experience, as well as an example of Christian service and commitment. Russell Boatman was the President, G. H. Cachairas was the Student Dean, as well as Professor of New Testament and Greek. Earl Grice was Academic Dean, and Professor of Theology. Don Riggin was Registrar, and Eulah Hall was Office Manager and Merel Maher, Assistant to the President. The rest of the teaching staff included, Howard Hayes, Professor of Church History, Ronald Keeler, Professor of English, Harold and Wilma Haskell, Professors of Homiletics and Speech, Lawrence Sunkler, Professor of Music, Mary Jane Cabus, Professor of Christian Education and I was the rookie Professor of Hebrew, Old Testament and Evangelism. We had faculty meetings on a weekly basis, usually conducted by the Academic Dean. We were expected to speak in chapel at least once each semester. We were men and women of diverse backgrounds, different personalities, and different gifts and educational skills. We complemented each other in a wonderful way, and proved to be an effective team for equipping young men and women for various areas of ministry. This is attested to by the tremendous impact Minnesota Bible College graduates have made for the cause of Christ through the years all over the world. I became very close friends to most of my colleagues, but Harold Haskell and Howard Hayes were closer to me than the others. Harold shared an office with me, so we were forced to spend much time together. However, Howard and I hit it off immediately. We were golf buddies, fellows students, and had common interests in the work of the church, and especially missions and evangelism. Not only did he attend classes with me at The University of Minnesota, but he also worked with me in helping to get a campus ministry started there. We shared some very interesting and humorous experiences. His wife Florence had a special gift of hospitality, and their children were models of what one would desire in a Bible college atmosphere.

## Spring Tour

One of the duties of each faculty and staff member was to participate in the annual Spring Tour. It was a time when we would travel with our students to the various churches that supported the college, either financially or by sending us students. It was a time for showing off our best and brightest and most talented students. It was a very demanding experience. We would travel day and night to get to the various appointments the college had made for us. We slept in all kinds of beds, ate all kinds of food, under all kinds of circumstances, with many different kinds of people. Due to the latter, I may write a book sometime entitled, "Beds I have slept in." Often times we would arrive just in time for the services to start, only to find that the preacher had forgotten to inform the people we were coming, because he had forgotten about it himself. He would get on the phone and scurry around to find accommodations for us. Even though this was a yearly tradition, and I took part in it for at least ten years, several of the tours, and several of the teams that traveled with me stand out in my memory more than the others. I can't remember for sure where I went that first year. However, I remember traveling with Paul Carrier, Bob Cash, Morris Fetty, and Stan Melton, all excellent representatives of Jesus Christ. What the College was attempting to accomplish, they have proven many times in the roles they have played in the preaching ministry and in Christian education.

One year I traveled with a girls trio consisting of Nancy Chapman, Cecelia McMurray, Jane Brown, and I believe Peggy Howard was our pianist. We were to drive from Minneapolis to Sullivan, Indiana, and give our presentation to the Christian Church there. Jack Anderson was the preacher at that time. It was Nancy Chapman's home church. We were supposed to be there in time to make our presentation at 7 P.M. Due to the many miles we would have to travel, we left Minneapolis at 4:30 A.M. We had traveled about one hundred miles when one of the girls informed me they had forgotten their dresses. We had to turn around and drive back to Minneapolis to get them, and then started back where we had just come from. We drove as fast as we could, however, with young women, that proved to not be very fast, as they needed to make rest stops about ever half hour or forty-five minutes. The roads were narrow black tops, with the average speed limit at fifty miles per hour. I am afraid I broke that limit many times in my effort to get to our engagement on time. However, that was to no avail as we finally arrived in Sullivan at 3:00 A.M. the next morning. We found out later that the church was packed with people, anxiously awaiting our presentation, singing hymns for more than an hour, and finally giving up on us and going home. It was a very embarrassing experience, but the most embarrassing was yet to come. The next morning, we met for breakfast in the home of the preacher, Jack Anderson. His wife had prepared a delicious breakfast. Due the distance we had to travel in order to make our next engagement, we had to be there for breakfast by 6:00 A.M. We were not about to be late again. I was barely awake when I sat down at that breakfast table. Our hostess had placed a beautiful white lace tablecloth on the table. In spite of the fact that we had missed our assignment with them, they treated us as though nothing had happened. I reached for the glass of milk she had placed on the table for me, but somehow misjudged where it was, and with one sweep of my arm, sent my glass flying with milk covering the beautiful white tablecloth. If at all possible I would have crawled under that table, as I can still see the shocked look on the face of Preacher Anderson's wife, as the milk came flooding down her beautifully set table. I wondered if it was all just a terrible nightmare, but the muffled laughs of my Gospel team soon dispelled that wishful thought.

The Spring Tours that I participated in took me as far East as West Virginia, and as far west as Montana, Wyoming, Colorado, New Mexico and Arizona. They also took me from Minnesota to Louisiana in the South. Some of the most memorable tours were the ones that took us to famous historical sights in Montana, Colorado and New Mexico. The tour in New

Mexico was particularly interesting, as between Taos and Albuquerque, New Mexico, we visited the famous Newspaper rock on the wall of a cliff in that area. In Montana, we followed the route of Louis and Clark, the famous explorers and viewed the headwaters of the Missouri River. We made a presentation in Fort Benton and also Lewistown, where my sister Suzanne was born, and where my father had coached football. The preacher at Lewistown was our long time friend and former class mate, Ron McConkey. I later came back and held special services for the church there. I should mention that we made our presentation in Havre, Montana before driving to Fort Benton. At that time, the preacher who spoke at my ordination in Goldfield, Iowa, Clayton Kent was the minister. My brother-in-law, Jack Rampelberg followed him there. He was our Forwarding Agent when we went to Africa. The thing I remember the most, outside of the fine Western hospitality afforded us in Montana, was the biting cold. The heater in our car didn't put out much heat, so we were cold all of the time. We were happy to go from there south to sunny Colorado. Our tour that

*Jerry with Dean Earl Grice at conference in Rochester, Minnesota*

took us south from Minnesota, through Arkansas, Texas and down to Louisiana, was also very memorable and providential, for from the first time we traveled there in 1958, I was invited back every summer by Hollins Duhon, minister of the church in Lake Charles and other ministers in Louisiana to hold special meetings, and to speak at their Christian service camp at Lake Arthur, just outside of Jennings. It was the Jennings Church that financed our trip to Beijing, China, under the ministry of Jack Harris. That church, as well as several individuals in that area have continued their support of our ministries through the years. We established precious friendships in Louisiana that we will cherish forever. Many, such as Hollins and René Duhon, and Dallas and Harry Guillory have gone on to their reward.

Also, while we were there, we visited the famous French Quarter in New Orleans for the first time. There we were introduced to dark roast coffee and hot, spicy Cajun food. Gumbo has now become a tradition with our family on special occasions like Thanksgiving or Christmas.

I want to make mention of some of the people who toured with me. A group of young ladies including, Maurice "Squeak" Butler, Pat and Sylvia Barker, and Pat Hasty traveled with us to Montana and also Colorado. Some of the young men who traveled with us both West and South were LeRoy Randall, Don Kooey, Tim Coop, Dick Henthorn, Bill Miller, Al Shoemaker, Jack Kirkland and David Bradshaw. I am sure there were others who I cannot recall at this time.

The group that I remember the best was the group I traveled with after returning from Africa. They called themselves "The Victors Quartet," consisting of Mike Knezivich, Larry Medcalf, Terry Fulk, John Patton, and I believe, Ken Waddel. I can close my eyes and hear them singing, "Without Him I can do nothing. . . ."

Bill Miller and I still have had many a chuckle over the time we traveled to Rowen, Iowa to speak at the Congregational Church there where Jack Rampelberg was a student preacher. I spoke for the morning worship hour, and Merle Mahor spoke at an afternoon rally. We sat down for a Sunday dinner with perhaps the most influential people in the church. I will not mention their names. Bill Miller and Al Shoemaker were with me. The main course meal was excellent. Now it was time for desert. Our hostess announced that she had prepared a dessert that she had never tried before. She asked us if we liked lemon pie. Of course, the three of us responded with a loud, "Yes!" It was an honest answer. She placed before each of us a piece of her masterpiece. It looked strangely orange. The first bite revealed why. She had made the meringue out of the egg yolk, rather than the egg white. It was awful. She asked us, "How do you like it?" That is like asking someone, "Am I as dumb as I look?" It was a no-win situation. We tried to tell her it was delicious, but the expressions on our faces told the lie. We tried to keep our composure, but to no avail. The three of us burst out with a peal of laughter at the same time. It was a nervous laughter. Needless to say, we were never invited back to her house for dinner.

As I now recall, that day was a bitter-sweet day. Normadeene's father and mother, Bert and Hattie Pletcher, drove over to Rowen from Clarion, to share in the Sunday afternoon program. Bert had not been well, and that afternoon he had a strange yellow look. Half way into the program, he got up and went outside. For some reason, I got up and followed him out. I did not have a part in the afternoon program, so I felt free to do so. When I got outside, there he was sitting in his old green Ford. I opened the passenger side door and climbed in next to him. I was raised at a time when it was not manly for men to express openly their love for one another. We never hugged or embraced. My own father never told me he loved me until he was ninety years old. Normadeene's father, for many years was closer to me than my own father. He loved me dearly. It seemed I had taken the place of the son he never had. I some time think that Normadeene's two brother-in-laws were a wee bit jealous of the special treatment he gave to me. He never scolded me, but only offered words of encouragement and good common sense advice. I may have mentioned earlier that I was so eager to win people to Christ, that often times I was not as patient as I should have been. It was Bert Pletcher who counseled me, "Start with people where you find them, not where you want them to be." As I look back, I realize that I was like a bull who carried his China closet with him. He was always there for us when we needed him. He opened his home, heart and pocketbook to Normadeene and me. As I sat there next to him, I felt very awkward and did not know where to begin. Finally in the midst of choked back tears, I expressed my love and appreciation to him. He cried. I cried. We hugged and both felt much better about life in general. However, it was a couple months later that I realized how important that precious moment with Dad Pletcher really was. Bert Pletcher, like my mother, made all of us children feel like we were very special, and we were to them. As I contemplate their love for their family and children, I call to mind the teachings of Dr. Watress. He introduced seven basic principles that he referred to as "The Seven A's," that were designed to help make our marriages and home life a little bit of heaven on earth. God intends for our homes to be the perfect pattern for the unity Jesus prayed for. "The Seven A's" are as follows:

1. *Acknowledgment*: Let our wives and children know how important they are to you. Spend time listening to them.
2. *Acceptance*: This is Year of Jubilee acceptance. Every fifty years, all debts were paid. Know their faults and still love them. Have a very short memory for wrongs done. I Cor. 13:5.
3. *Approval*: Gives a pat on the back along with words of encouragement.
4. *Appreciation*: Expresses love and thanksgiving while people are still living. The magic word "Thank you!"
5. *Admiration*: Admires special talents and gifts and expresses it often, especially in regard to special achievements.
6. *Adoration*: Words are nice, but actions are much better. It is possible to give without loving, but it is impossible to love without giving. John 3:16
7. *Infinite Affection*: Willing to die, "As Christ loved the church and gave Himself for her." Romans 5:8 Husbands must "die" for their wives when they marry them, just as Christ died for him. In turn, wives must submit themselves to their husbands to show love for them. They do it for God's sake.

Normadeene's father and my mother demonstrated these principles by the lives they lived. If you get nothing else out of reading this book, if you learn and practice these principles, it is worth it.

## And Then There Were Four

Many of the churches we visited on Spring Tour invited me back to conduct special services for them. One of them was the Council Bluffs Church of Christ in Council Bluffs, Iowa. It was the home church of Denny Ganz' wife, "Porky" Oliver. We were invited to speak on the week end of the sixteenth of April. Normadeene was carrying Becky at the time, and after several false alarms, the doctor said that Becky most likely would not be born until the first of May, possibly on my Birthday, May 4th. Normadeene started having labor pains early the morning of the 16th, the very morning of the day I was to drive to Council Bluff with a girls trio, for an Area-Wide Youth Rally. I rushed her to the Swedish Hospital in Minneapolis. Once again, we were told it was a false alarm. I was to teach my Job class from 9:30 A.M. until 10:30 A.M. I was assured that Normadeene would not deliver Becky until that class was over, and I would have plenty of time to be there by her side when Becky decided she wanted to be born. So, reluctantly, I left and met my Job class. Somehow, I felt uneasy about the whole situation, so I dismissed my class early, and rushed back to the hospital. When I entered Normadeene's room, she was cradling Becky in her arms. That beautiful baby girl could not wait. So there she was waiting for me.

I hated to leave Normadeene and our darling Becky to speak at that Youth Rally in Council Bluffs. However, Normadeene urged me to fulfill my obligation, as she reminded me that all those young people at the Youth Rally would be waiting to hear me speak. Also, the girls trio was counting on me to get them there, as they were the special music for the rally. You can understand what I meant when I expressed my gratitude and deep admiration for the dedication, and willingness to sacrifice on the part of Normadeene. Many women would have done just the opposite and complained bitterly if their husbands left them at such a time in their lives. I often wonder now, if I had my priorities right, because as I have said before, I am convinced that outside of our relationship with Jesus Christ, family is the next most important thing in our lives.

I mentioned Havre, Montana as one of the churches we visited on Spring Tour. I had held several revivals in the Kimball, Minnesota Church of Christ the first couple of years I was a professor at Minnesota Bible College. Kimball was a little more than one-hundred miles from Minneapolis. I would drive to Kimball in the afternoon, and drive back after the evening services. A young man from the church, Lee Hoskins, would ride back with me. That helped to keep me awake. Clayton Kent was the minister there, but accepted a call to the Sixth Avenue Christian Church in

Havre in 1957. As I mentioned earlier, he was minister of the Goldfield, Iowa Church of Christ where I was ordained into the ministry. Clayton wanted the men of the Sixth Avenue Christian Church to hear me, so he invited me to come for a week-end of preaching as a warm up for their revival. I asked to bring our youngest son, G.A. with me, as he was only four years old, and was not yet in school. And also, because he missed me so much when I was gone. I had awakened from sound sleep several times, only to find him standing over me, with his blanket in his arms, just staring at me. My schedule at the college caused me to be gone when he woke up in the morning, and I did not get home before he went to bed. On one occasion, he was siting with Normadeene and thoughtfully said to her, "Do you remember my daddy? He's nice."

*MBC's yearbook dedicated to the Gibson family*

In those days we traveled by train. I had a Clergy Pass that gave special fares to preachers. The trains were pulled by large steam engines. Some times two or three engines were hooked together in order to pull the weight of the train, especially in mountainous areas. I booked a very nice roomette for G.A. and myself. It was a self-contained compartment with a toilet, sink, and bed that folded down from the ceiling. We took our meals in the dining car. That was an adventure in itself, as well as a very enjoyable experience. The food was delicious and the service was excellent. A black porter was usually in charge. We did not have a lot of money, so this was a extra treat for us, as we didn't eat like that very often at home. This was in January of 1959. It took about eighteen hours for the train to travel from Minneapolis to Havre, we would board the train about 6 P.M. We would get a good nights rest while the train was traveling over some of the most boring landscape in America, and then wake up for breakfast the next morning, and arrive in Havre late that afternoon. What a thrill to pull into the depot and find Clayton Kent and several other men from the church waiting there for us. They rolled out the purple carpet for us. We had never been treated as royalty before. On the night I was to bring my first message, G.A. was to be a part of the program. At four years old I had taught him the Hebrew alphabet! Clayton Kent was interested in learning Hebrew. I told him how the students at the Bible College complained when I asked them to learn the Hebrew alphabet the first week of our Hebrew class. I would invite G.A. into the class the next day and have him stand up in front of the class and rattle off the alphabet. The next day the class knew the Hebrew alphabet. Clayton asked G.A. to recite the Hebrew alphabet. He stood up front of a packed auditorium and starting with aleph, he went through all twenty-two let-ters of the Hebrew alphabet without missing a consonant. The last night of the meetings, they called him up to the front and presented him with a cowboy hat and cowboy boots. He was one happy preacher's kid that evening. Before we left Havre, to return to Minneapolis, the men of the church booked me for a revival the second two weeks of June. Out of all of this, there came some hard feelings on the part of my mother-in-law. She thought I showed favoritism to G.A. over the rest of our children. The reason I took G.A. with me is because Gibby and Cindy were in school. And they could not afford to miss any classes. Perhaps, if I had to do it over again, I would make more of an effort to let them know how impor-tant they were to me. I took for granted they knew that. However, hind-sight is always better than foresight. Minnesota Bible College was closed during the summer months, so we were free to spend time on our own holding meetings, etc. However, we were obligated to represent the col-lege at Christian service camps, and speak on behalf of the college to sup-porting churches. We arrived in Havre, for their summer revival the first weekend in June, 1959. We left Gibby and Cindy with Grandma Pletcher, and had G.A. and two-and-a-half-month-old Becky with us. It was a long drive from Minneapolis to Havre. We marveled at the awesome railroad bridge in Jamestown, North Dakota, and enjoyed driving through Glendive, and viewing the Fort Peck Dam in Montana. We thought of the history surrounding the places we drove through and commented how it must have been for the pioneers who settled that part of our country. Custer's Massacre took place at The Little Big Horn in Southern Montana. We imagined Native Americans, lurking in the rocks, as we traveled through the territory that once was theirs. We stayed with Hershel and Alice Fox, out on their ranch. They treated us like honored members of their family. They had two children who we had met earlier in Minneapolis at the Bible college. We celebrated our Tenth Wedding Anniversary, on June 13th, there in Havre. However, what ordinarily was a time for celebration and rejoicing, turned into a time of sorrow and mourning. Normadeene's father, Bert Pletchers, took a turn for the worse, and went to be with King Jesus on our wedding anniversary. Never in our lives had we experienced the kind of love and compassion shown to us by the Sixth Avenue Christian Church in Havre. They chartered an airplane that flew us out to the funeral and back. We took G.A. with us, but felt Becky was too young for that trip, so left her in the loving arms of Hershel and Alice Fox.

I mentioned how I expressed to Normadeene's father, that Sunday afternoon in Rowan, Iowa, how much I loved him, and how much I appreciated him as my father-in-law. I sat there in the Church in Clarion, Iowa, where his funeral was conducted, and watched people pass by the open casket, viewing his mortal remains for the last time. Some of them went so far as to hug his dead body. Many of them had not spoken to him for years and had never expressed their love for him. I praised and thanked God, that I didn't wait until he was dead to say, "Thank you, and tell him I loved him!" Normadeene was a "Daddy's Girl" and misses him deeply. However, she does not sorrow as those who have no hope, as she knows where Bert Pletcher is. I Thessalonians 4:13. If there is somebody you love dearly, but have not said so lately, please, right now, put this book down and get on the phone, or on e-mail, and don't let another hour go by, before you tell them, "I love you, and thank you for being you." Calvin Milan, one of my graduating class of 1950 at Minnesota Bible College, conducted the victory celebration for Normadeene's father. When we arrived back in Montana, early one morning, Hershel Fox decided to take us to "The Going to the Sun Highway" in Glacier National Park. To get there we went through Cut Bank, which became famous due to a world-champion boxing match between Gene Tuney and Jack Dempsey. As we started up the mountain, we were thrilled by the magnificent scenery we were beholding. Living in Minnesota and Iowa, where a small hill is considered a mountain, caused us to have tremendous love and appreciation for the real mountains that we were now traveling. There was a rushing, roaring stream by the side of the road that added much to the beauty we were trying to contain. We have never ceased being amazed by the handiwork of God that could produce such wonders of nature. We were busy enjoying the wonder of it all, when all of the sudden, a big black bear loomed up in front of us just off of the highway. We were fascinated at the sight! Hershel Fox had brought his 8mm movie camera with him, and I had a little cheap Kodak Pony. The bear just stood there and posed for us. I had some candy orange slices in a bag that I had brought along for a snack. I said to Normadeene, "Why don't you get out of the car, and while I lure the bear with orange slices, you take a picture of him." She looked a little bit shocked at first, but I assured her there was nothing to fear from that fine, gentle, tame bear. She stepped out of the car, but while she was trying to focus on the bear, the bear decided to get a little closer, and started towards her. She did not see it coming. I yelled, "Normadeene! Get back in the car!" She looked up and saw the bear coming after her. For a moment, she froze. She said it was like in a dream when you tried to run, but could not move. Then, for a quick moment, she gained her composure and <u>barely</u> escaped back into the car. In the mean time, I was shaking the bag of candy orange slices at the bear. I took one out of the bag and was going to throw it to him. However, there was one big problem. (Incidentally, Hershell Fox was getting all of this on his moving picture camera.) I had forgotten to roll my window all of the way up. In a moment, the greedy bear was half way into the front seat of the car, on my lap, wanting to have the whole bag of candy orange slices. I did not argue with him, but let him have them immediately.

Once while in Yosemite, we were sleeping in a small pup-tent at the foot of El Capitan. We both had our own sleeping bags. In the middle of the night Normadeene woke me up and said she felt something wet on her toes. I shined our flashlight, and there stood a big brown bear at the door of our tent. My sleeping bag was zipped up. But somehow Normadeene was able to get into my sleeping bag without it being unzipped. Fortunately for us, the bear turned his attention to a camper that was near by.

He had picked up a cooler and was shaking it to get it open. The men in the camper opened the door to the back of their camper to see what was happening. When they saw the bear, they didn't take time to break camp, but went roaring away. We didn't see them again while we were there.

The Sixth Avenue Christian Church in Havre, Montana, was destined to play a major roll in our ministries to come. We still keep in touch with the Foxes and several other members of the church there.

Spring Tour continued to be a source of door openings for me to hold revivals and conduct special services in the churches we had been in. The Lewistown, Montana church's preacher, Ron McConkey asked me to hold a two-week revival for his church in June. I was delighted to respond that we would come. I previously mentioned, my father had been a teacher and coach there in the early twenties, and my sister Suzanne was born there. She was born on March 13, 1923. We were to stay with the McConkey's in the parsonage. We had three children with us, Gibby, Cindy and G.A., and I believe they had two children. That made for a pretty full house. Ron's wife, Lois, was an excellent host, and an example of what it means to be a "Christian" wife and mother. She was an excellent minister's wife. We had some very interesting experiences with our children invading the McConkey household, and hearing the McConkey kids exclaiming, "That's mine!" as our children attempted to take over their playthings. However, all in all, under the cramped quarters and other extenuating circumstances, our children and their children adjusted very well to each other and became close friends. I do recall that one of the McConkey children had to be rushed to the emergency room. It seems that G.A. *accidentally* hit them over the head with a blunt object. So many wonderful things happened during our revivals, that it is difficult to pick out any one thing, as God always poured down blessings beyond our capacity to contain. However, one experience there in Lewistown, stands out above all others.

One of the very interesting and often adventurous things we did at our revivals was to eat lots of food at many different tables. We were scheduled by the Hospitality Committee to take meals at noon and dinner time. That was quite an undertaking for those who provided this very wonderful, but necessary hospitality. At times, I would ask to take my meals after the evening service, as our afternoon calling on prospects for the church often took us up into the dinner hour, and we would barely get back in time for the evening service. People would remind us on the way out of the evening service, that they were expecting us in their home for a meal. It was like feeding a small army, as we were like locusts. We came in swarms, and ate everything in sight. I suggested to the man of the household we were to be at for an evening meal, that if it would be all right with them, I would rather eat after the service. It was not because I would be late making calls, as much as the fact that often times I would be back in the pulpit in less than an hour after I had eaten. I told him that I could preach better if my stomach was not so full. As he walked out of the church that night, he shook my hand, grinned and said, "You might as well have et."

One of our noon meals was at the home of Mr. and Mrs. Greeves. I can not recall their first names. Mr. Greeves was ninety-two years old, and Mrs. Greeves was his second wife. She was only seventy-five. She was a devout Christian and was at the church whenever its doors were open. She never missed a service if she could help it. She took very seriously the admonition of Hebrews 10:25,26. Her husband, on the other hand, never darkened the doorway of the church. She had pled with him and begged him in every way she could think of, to accompany her to church, but to no avail. Ron McConkey always tried to prepare me for any eventuality that may take place in the homes we were to be in. He took special care to fill me in on the situation with old Mr. Greeves. It seemed that he had spent hours with Mr. Greeves with no visible success, and he went on tell me that, "Every evangelist who has ever been here has tried to get him into the water," referring to his need to be baptized. I immediately thought, "That is a big part of the problem." We should not be interested in getting people into the baptistry, but into a personal relationship with Jesus Christ. Ron urged and cautioned me not to get into any kind of theological discussion with that old man, as he has all of the answers, and particularly, do not bring up the subject of baptism. I assured him that I would comply with his advice. We arrived a little bit early at the Greeves home. We were greeted warmly by Mrs. Greeves and ushered into their living room. Mr. Greeves had recently fallen and broken his hip, and was in a wheelchair. He grunted a welcome to us all. As I sat down, to my chagrin, Ron, Lois and Normadeene headed for the kitchen and left me there alone with Mr. Greeves. I had made a covenant with my mouth before entering his home, so I sat there and waited for him to start a conversation. I didn't have to wait long, for to my dismay, that old gentleman proceeded to recount his days as a young man in Montana, and his personal experience with the Nez-Perce, crooked noses, Native Americans. He had met Chief Joseph who led the Trail of Tears as his people were forced to wander from their homeland. He remembered every detail. I sat there spellbound. It was like I was reliving all of his experiences with him. I finally broke in and exclaimed, "Mr. Greeves, you need to write this down in a book! Otherwise it will be lost." He looked me in the eye and to my surprise asked me, "Do you think I should be baptized? I have been thinking about it." I had not said a thing. I said, "Jesus commanded it." And I quoted Mark 16:6. He then turned toward the kitchen and shouted to his wife, "Honey! I'm going to be baptized!" They all came running from the kitchen. They had surprised looks and wondered what I had said. I assured them that it was all his idea. It is surprising how people's attitude change when the circumstances change. All of Mr. Greeves' relatives claim to have been praying that he would make such a decision. But now that he had declared himself, suddenly they were more interested in his physical well being than his spiritual well being. They started to find reasons why he should not be baptized. "He is an old man and his heart couldn't stand the shock." Also, "He is recovering from a broken hip, and there is no way he can get in and out of that baptistry." I assured his friends and family that God's strong hand would be upon him. I told them we will place a chair in the baptistry and strong men will place him down onto the chair. The minister would simply bend the chair backwards, and then strong men would lift him up out of the baptistry. I don't often do the baptizing at a revival. I believe it is important for the local minister to establish a close relationship with his people. Baptisms, weddings and such like, are excellent opportunities for that to happen. So, unless it is the specific request of the candidate, I insist that the local preacher does the baptizing. Mr. Greeves desired me to baptize him, to which I gladly complied. And Ron McConkey had no problem with that, as like the rest of us, he was thankful that he desired to be baptized. Mr. and Mrs. Greeves were together in the church for the first time that evening. He sat in his wheelchair. When the invitation was given for people to make decisions for Christ, Mr. Greeves rolled forward in his wheel chair. Ron took his confession of faith, and when he was in the baptistry, I said to him, "Mr. Greeves, because of the confession of your faith that Jesus is the Christ, the Son of the Living God, and because Jesus commanded it, you are now being baptized into Jesus, in the name of the Father, and Son and Holy Spirit for the remission of your sins, and the indwelling presence of the Holy Spirit, and the promise of everlasting life!" I then lowered him and the chair backwards under the water, and "raised him to walk in newness of life." People were standing by anxious to see if there had been any ill effect on him. They said, "How do you feel?" His answer is still ringing in my ears. He took a deep breath, and then, with a loud, clear, strong, voice, shouted, "I feel wonderful! I feel wonderful! I only wish I had not waited so long." I asked him later why he agreed to be baptized now, when he had resisted so many preachers before. He said, "All of the other preachers did all of the talking. They did not listen to me. You listened to me. Now, I was ready to listen to you." Sometimes people just need somebody who will listen to them. Then God will speak to their hearts. I will always cherish the memory of Mr. Greeves and our revival in Lewistown, Montana.

## Chapter XVIII
### OTHER MEMORABLE EXPERIENCES

There were a couple of other revivals that stand out in my mind, that I believe had some very special situations and circumstances and victories that I should share with you. One was at The Billings Creek Church of Christ in the Wildcat Mountains of Wisconsin, and the other was at Oelwein, Iowa.

Morris Fetty was one of my very talented students from Viroqua, Wisconsin. He had a weekend ministry in a little country church, Billings Creek Church of Christ, nestled in the hills of the Wildcat Mountains. I held a revival for him at Billings Creek one summer in the late fifties. I often wonder if I had known the circumstances and living conditions I would be facing, would I have agreed to hold that meeting. I don't have to wonder very long, though, because I believed very strongly that little, struggling churches, like the Billings Creek Church, should have the opportunity to hear good preaching as much as the larger, more successful churches do. I was young and had lots of energy, but most of all, a tremendous passion for souls. At that time in his life, so did Morris Fetty.

After the first service on Sunday evening, we were taken to the place we were to stay during the revival. About ten people were living there in very cramped quarters. There was no bedroom for us, and no bed, and no privacy, and no indoor plumbing! There was a davenport in the living room that had enough room for one person to sleep, but we were told that we both had to sleep there. There was no place to hang our clothes, and only a wash basin in the master bedroom for bathing. I was a very private person at that time, and I immediately became very nervous about our situation. My hair always gets very messed up when I sleep and I hate to have people, especially those who are not in my immediate family, see me that way. There was not even a mirror. We were to take our meals with various church families, and after considering our situation where we were staying, I had visions of the situation I found myself in at another revival. I walked into the house through the kitchen and there on the kitchen table were chickens scratching in the dough that was left from the biscuits our host had just put in the oven. There was a strong smell of cat urine that made me gag, and there were a few piles of cat dung here and there. My host didn't seem to think anything about it. This was normal for her. The last thing I want to do, is to sound like a snob or a prude. However, I still believe in the Proverb that proclaims that "Cleanliness is next to Godliness." Many gracious Christians that have hosted me through the years, who were of meager means, presented a clean and well kept house, and served a common, but delicious meal. My fears

*A revival bulletin*

were soon dispelled, because every home we ate in provided excellent food in a very healthy setting. The people in that church were poor, but they were gracious and shared with us what they had.

I might inject here, that on one occasion, I stayed in a home where I had to walk through the Master bedroom to go to the bathroom. And on another occasion, not too long ago, I was put in a room that served as the playroom for the children. It had no bed clothes, and I had to remove the toys from off of the bed in order to get into it. But the real difficult thing for me was the bathroom. The bathtub had a bucket of very dirty and stinky diapers in it. The smell of that also made me gag. The door to the bathroom was next to the kitchen and it could not be closed. The children would barge right in on me while I was going to the bathroom, or washing or shaving. I would do it all over again, because the satisfaction of seeing people come to a saving knowledge of Jesus Christ is always well worth any sacrifice one might have to make. Normadeene and I stayed in a place where we slept in the basement on an old uncovered mattress that belonged to the family dog. The surprising thing is, that in the case of many of the people we have stayed with, seeing them in church, you would never dream what it was like in their homes.

I apologize for allowing myself to get sidetracked. However, I believe it will help you to appreciate more what God's servants have to endure in order to carry out Jesus' Great Commission.

A teen age girl who was in Morris' youth group had been attending our revival each night. One night she got home a little later than usual. Her father met her at the door and demanded to know where she had been to get home so late. After she told him that she had been to our revival, he demanded that she never go back to that church. He went on to say that if he ever met up with that preacher, he would beat him up! Word of this, somehow got back to Morris. Her father was a big rough man, and Morris did not relish the thought of tangling with him.

Morris made a list of people he considered to be prospects for becoming Christians, and also for people who were Christians, to join fellowship with the Billings Creek Church. We made every call on his list—except for the father of the teen age girl who was going to beat Morris up if he saw him. I told Morris that we owed it to the girl to go out and talk to her father. She had also expressed her desire to be baptized sometime during our revival. She certainly could not fulfill that desire if her father refused her permission to attend our evening service. This was on a Friday afternoon. It would be our only opportunity, as I would be returning to Minneapolis on Saturday morning. I convinced Morris that we must, at least, try to get to her father and reason with him. He reluctantly agreed with me, and we started out to his farm. We had gone about a mile when Morris asked me to pull over to the side of the road and pray. I did. I prayed that God would take away any fear from Morris' heart, quoting II Timothy 1:7, and asking God to touch the heart of the teen age girl's father. That seemed to renew Morris courage, so we went on our way. However, a few miles down the road, Morris asked me to pull over to the side of the road again and pray some more. That repeated itself four times before we reached our destination. As we pulled into the drive way, we saw a very interesting sight. There, stuck in the kitchen door, was the girl's father. He had been trying to move a large refrigerator into the kitchen, but got stuck in the door. The timing was perfect. We offered our assistance. We freed him and the refrigerator and helped him place it where he wanted it to be in the kitchen. He then turned and ordered his daughter to start getting ready to attend our revival that night, and promised to be there himself. God works in wondrous ways to accomplish his will in our lives. That evening, the young lady was baptized into Christ. Not long after that, her father and other members of her family became Christians. So you can well see that the satisfaction we received was well worth any sacrifice we might have made.

The last revival experience I want to relate to you, while we were with Minnesota Bible College, was in Oelwein, Iowa. We were invited to hold special services at the Oelwein Church of Christ during a time when they did not have a minister. Several years before, Normadeene had helped conduct Daily Vacation Bible School. She stayed with a wonderful old lady, Grandma Staples. We stayed with her during this revival. Half way through the first week of what was to be a one-week revival, I stopped by the local drug store and noticed some golf balls resting by the cash register. I inquired of the sales person, who turned out to be the proprietor, "Who do those golf balls belong to?" He told me they were his and that he loved the game of golf. I introduced myself to him, and invited him and his family to attend our revival service. He asked me if I played golf. I told him I did and that I happened to have my golf clubs in the trunk of my car. He asked me if I would play golf with him some morning while I was there. I agreed to do so, if he agreed to attend our revival. He agreed to, so and we met the next morning at the local golf course. I am convinced that angels guided my golf clubs and golf balls that morning. I had never hit the ball that far or that straight. My drug store owner friend was amazed. As he had agreed, he and his family attended the revival services that evening. He hung on every word I spoke that night. As he walked out of the door, he told me that he had several business men friends who had never seen a person play golf as he witnessed from me that morning. He asked if I would agree to play a round of golf with them. I agreed, but only if they would also attend our revival services. He contacted his friends, and they agreed to that condition.

Once again, angels must have guided my golf clubs and golf ball. We came to a hole that was a par five. It was a dogleg over a small lake. If one could cut the corner and drive his ball over that lake, he would only have a short chip onto the green and a putt for an eagle. I did not intend to drive my ball over the lake. However, man proposes, but God disposes, because I hooked my ball, and to my dismay, and the unbelief of my newly found business men friend, I hit the ball over the lake with room to spare. I ended up with a rare eagle on that hole.

As we walked down the fairways, the men started asking me questions about the Bible. It finally led to the question, "What must I do to be saved?" I ended up taking the drug store owner's confession of faith in Jesus Christ as the Son of God on the seventeenth green. I had the joy of baptizing him into Christ that evening. We were supposed to be there for one week. The men of the church asked us if we could possibly stay for an extra week. The little railroad town was buzzing over what was happening at our revival and also the young professor from Minnesota Bible College of whom it was said, "He can hit a golf ball a mile!" It would pose no problem for me, but Normadeene was my song leader, and she had left our children with her folks, and was anxious to get back to them. However, she agreed to stay another week, after talking to her mother on the phone. After the second week, which brought many people to Christ, the men approached us again and asked if we could stay for a third week. I agreed to do so, but Normadeene had to get back to our children. I agreed to lead the singing as well as do the preaching each night. When we finished that third week, they still wanted more. That was good, because I have told my students through the year, "When you speak, always leave them wanting more."

As I look back to those days when revivals were an anticipated part of church life, two-week meetings being the norm, I wonder about several things. We jokingly used to say of the length of a revival meeting. "A one-week meeting is *one weak* meeting. A two-week meeting is *too weak*." I also wonder how I could call on prospects all day long and preach every night for three weeks. Where did I get that many evangelistic sermons to preach? You did not dare have dull messages, because you would lose your crowd. People get bored if the message does not meet the needs in their lives. I have often remarked, "People go to church Lord's Day after Lord's Day, expecting to hear nothing, and they are seldom disappointed." It has been said by modern theologians, "The day where preaching is effective is over." My reply is, "The kind of preaching they are talking about has been over a long time ago." However, "It still pleases God through the foolishness of preaching to save those who believe." Not foolish preaching, but preaching that reveals the mystery that God chose a rugged cross to reconcile man to Himself. I Corinthians 1:21

What I have shared with you is but a small representation of the many revivals Normadeene and I conducted while we were still teaching at Minnesota Bible College. We now wish we had kept a journal of all of the churches we have shared the Gospel with, all of the tables we have eaten at, and all of the beds we have slept in both in America and abroad.

The best is still yet to come! Save your fork.

# *Chapter XIX*
## OUR BLESSED FAMILY AND THE FLYING DOLLAR

I had the privilege of baptizing all four of our children into Christ. I cannot overemphasize the importance of family in every area of our lives. Each child was very much involved in our ministry. Being a preacher's kid and a professor's kid put special demands on them. People seem to have a double standard for preacher's kids. Unfortunately, we didn't have classes on how to be a mother or father, nor did our role models. So we did the best we knew how to do at the time.

We raised and disciplined our children on the basis of the knowledge we possessed at the time. Because our knowledge was limited, we made errors in judgment. However, as I look back, I don't believe we made errors of heart. We always did what we thought was best for them at the time. Hindsight is always better than foresight. We made mistakes, but remember, "The past is not to be lived in, but learned by." That's what Walter Hagen meant when I caddied for him. He said, "Young man, the only shot that is important is the next shot." People often have a difficult time getting past their past. Even though our children were born of the same parents, same household, same problems and difficulties to face in their everyday lives, they had distinct personalities and special talents.

I have often been asked, "If you had it to do over again, what would you do different?" If we had it to do over again, we would teach them to fall madly in love with themselves. We'd have them admire themselves in front of a mirror as a person made in God's image, being very valuable to Him. John 3:16 proves that. We'd urge them to be themselves. And we'd give them the kind of acceptance and approval they would need in order to do that. Building up self-image is so important! My job, as a husband and father, is to motivate my wife and children to feel good about themselves. That's why the fourth through the tenth commandments are all about "loving our neighbors as ourselves." Exodus 20 and Leviticus 19:18. Our neighbor begins with those in our own immediate family.

God blessed Normadeene and me with four beautiful children: Joseph, Cindy, G.A., and Becky. We had many wonderful and joy-filled experiences as they grew up. A fine example of that is Becky. She was born in Minneapolis, Minnesota at Swedish Hospital on April 16, 1959. We named her Rebecca Joan. Of all our children, we were able to spend more time with her, as she was our last, and also she loved to travel with us. We traveled thousands of miles with her in the back seat of our car. We'd wake Becky up. She'd go to the bathroom, and often without getting fully dressed, clad in her pajamas, carrying her security blanket, she'd crawl into the back seat, curl up, and go sound to sleep.

Becky most always got along well with our three other children; however, the usual sibling rivalry was evident at the time. She was their baby sister, and they watched over her. Becky was tenderhearted. We knew all of her friends on a personal basis, as I baptized most of them, and all of them found a place at our dinner table for many a Sunday dinner. In fact, one of her friends, who is now a very successful businesswoman, wrote to tell us that the most memorable times in her teens were the times she was at our house for dinner.

Becky graduated from high school and enrolled at Illinois University. She majored in speech communication and minored in art. She is a very fine artist. Some of our favorite pictures on our walls are those she painted. She was initiated into the Gamma Phi Beta sorority, and moved into their house. She was elected president of the sorority for her senior year, and she made a tremendous impact on the other girls. I had the opportunity to offer the blessing at several of their special dinners.

One time during spring break, Becky and a group of her sorority friends drove to Florida. I had purchased a used Chevrolet, as big as a tank, and given it to her for her trip. I had checked it out as thoroughly as

I could but, unfortunately, that was not good enough. On the way back home, Becky called us late at night to tell us the car had broken down out in the middle of nowhere on one of the Interstates. She was able to get the car towed to an Amoco service station. She said some creepy guys were staring at them and giving them an uneasy feeling. I asked to speak to the manager. He agreed to accept my credit card over the phone, and made the necessary repairs to get the girls back on the road, and on their way home.

After Becky graduated, she took a job in Chicago, selling papers. She left there and moved to Minneapolis, and became a food service manager for a new Radison Inn Hotel. She found herself working long, tiresome hours for a boss that was impossible to please. She then took a job with Cardinal Strich University, headquartered in Milwaukee, Wisconsin, as a student recruiter. She was promoted rapidly, and was able to receive her master's degree in business management. Normadeene and I were there for her graduation. She was honored by being asked to present the keynote address. Her thesis subject was on attitude, We were very proud of her as she made an excellent presentation.

Mark Henricksen, a wonderful man, who also graduated from the University of Illinois, became Becky's best friend. He got his degree in forestry. When they married we couldn't have asked for a better person to be Becky's husband. God sent two beautiful daughters to this union, Laura and Carly. Carly was named in honor of both her grandfather Charles Henricksen and her grandmother Charlotte Gibson. Becky was carrying her at the time my mother passed away. We were so glad that Mark got to meet my mother while she was still alive. I believe Becky told my mother she was going to name her baby after them. I am convinced that Mark and Becky's marriage was arranged in heaven.

Becky was closest in age to her brother G.A. I was honored because he was named after me! Gerald Arthur Gibson Jr. was born in Macomb, Illinois, May 12, 1954. When he was young, everybody called him G.A., but like me, he goes by the name of Jerry. One morning I woke up and found Jerry standing over me with his blanket in his hand, seeing that I didn't get away in the morning, before he was awake. I made a concerted effort to spend more time with him, and even take him with us on long trips when possible.

Jerry was interested in sports. He followed the Minnesota Twins base-ball team and attended a World Series game with me. I gave him a baseball signed by the Twins' World Series team. Jerry also had a special love for football at a very early age. There was a Pee Wee League in our neighbor-hood when we lived at Crystal New Hope. At that time Jerry was big for his age and he was tough. He helped lead his team to the championship finals in his division. He played his heart and guts out in every game. I think that stuck with him a long time. He continued to play baseball, and we cherish a photo of him in his baseball uniform.

Jerry is very charismatic and has always had a charming personality. At both high school and college he worked hard and was commended for his dependability.

One time we went camping in Rocky Mountain National Park, just outside of Estes Park, Colorado. We took a picture of Jerry standing in front of the old police station, on what is now the Pearl Street Mall, with his friend John Upp. I specifically remember driving into Boulder, to bring the two of them back to our campsite, when we encountered a large herd of elk blocking the highway. Being from Illinois, that was quite a sight to behold. Jerry reminds me often that the steak I cooked that evening, over an open charcoal fire, was one oft most delicious he has ever eaten.

After Jerry graduated from high school he went to an excellent new school, Colorado Mountain College in Glenwood Springs, about thirty miles from Aspen. We were able to rent a nice little cabin for him at the Bar-B ranch, and he was delighted. As we left we did lots of praying. Jerry fit in well, and soon became a member of the college ski team. He was downhill racing when he hit a mogul that caused him to fall and break his leg just above the ankle. His foot turned outward, and he had much pain. He was told he would never be able to ski again. That was a big blow to him.

At the University of Illinois I discussed his situation with several of the football players who lived in our campus house. Jeff Hollenbach, our quarterback, suggested we see the team surgeon, as he had helped a lot of players with similar injuries. We prayed about it, as that doctor was very busy, and it was difficult to get an appointment with him. The prayer worked, because I was able to speak with him the first time I called. He said, "Come over right now, and I will take a look at your son's leg." We were there in a matter of minutes. That was on Friday afternoon. He told us to be at the hospital on Monday morning and he would see what he could do. He was able to straighten out Jerry's leg and today it is as good as it could possibly be, and he skis whenever he has the opportunity.

He transferred to Southern Illinois University in Carbondale. He did well at SIU and was able to maintain a grade point average that would qualify him to enroll at the University of Illinois in Champaign-Urbana for his junior year. He was majoring in political science.

After Jerry graduated from the University of Illinois he worked with Continental Airlines, whose headquarters were in Houston. He became vice president of the Cargo Division. Working there he made the maiden nonstop flight from Houston to Tokyo, Japan.

While with Continental he met his wife, Kenna Wharf. I had the privilege of officiating at their wedding, at the Boulder Valley Christian Church, in Colorado. They had the reception at the Boulderado Hotel, a beautifully refurbished historical landmark. Jerry has an excellent job now with a consulting firm.

We are proud to have a wonderful son like Jerry and such a beautiful, loving daughter-in-law like Kenna. They are both very special people who are making their mark on this world.

Jerry and his older sister Cindy were both born at Saint Frances Hospital in Macomb, Illinois. Cynthia Charlotte was born November 12, 1951. Cindy and Jerry were very close. They fought a lot, especially while traveling in our car, but they loved each other dearly. They made up games to play, and had special stories about a Goosh-ball that they fantasized, and they often sang songs together in the car. Cindy always had a tremendous imagination for making up stories.

For Cindy high school was the time to leave the nest and get out on her own. She probably was the prototype of American youth in the sixties and seventies. The miracle took place after she moved to Chicago and was living in Rogers Park. She had a good job as a waitress in a swanky restaurant, and she tells of how she dumped a whole bowl of spaghetti down the neck of one of the customers. The tarnished customer had a sense of humor, so everybody got a good laugh out of it. Normadeene and I worried about Cindy because we had not heard from her for quite some time. We decided to surprise her and drive to Chicago and visit her. We had her

*Jerry and Normadeene's fiftieth wedding anniversary family picture*

address but hadn't been in that part of Chicago. As we drove down the street that approaches the address we had for her apartment, we stopped at a stop sign and looked across the street. There was Cindy just about to board a bus for downtown Chicago. Had we been there five seconds later, we may never have found her.

We received a call from Florida in the middle of the night. It was Kenny Dureon, asking my permission to marry Cindy. They were married in our living room on Florida Avenue in Urbana, with me taking their vows. To this union, God brought Melissa, our third granddaughter, into the world. Kenny drowned in a boating accident near his hometown, New Iberia, Louisiana. His death was a tragedy. At that time, Cindy and Missy, as we lovingly call her, were with us at Mid-South Christian College, where I was the president.

Cindy was the food service manager for the college and, also, was taking a full load of classes. She became famous for the delicious meals she cooked. Normadeene and Cindy received their associate of arts degrees in Christian education while we were there. Before we left Mid-South Christian College to move to Colorado, Cindy enrolled in Lincoln Christian College. There she made a mark for herself. She graduated with the highest honors in her class. I was given the honor of presenting Cindy with her degree. As I handed the degree to her she let out a resounding "Hallelujah!" That rocked the auditorium and brought down the house with laughter.

Cindy was hired as a drug abuse prevention specialist for the State of Illinois. Her boss was the son of Winston Zastrow, the man who sang "The Old Rugged Cross" at Mr. Beck's baptism in Stillwater Penitentiary. She was so good at her job that she was asked on several occasions to address the Illinois legislature.

While attending Lincoln Christian College she met Wayne Vale. They were an excellent match. I had the privilege of officiating at their wedding in Lincoln. Wayne had two children from a previous marriage. Cindy and Wayne are both devout Christians. Cindy stands tall in her knowledge of the Bible and her faithfulness to its precepts. Cindy and Wayne reside in Des Moines, Iowa. They are not far from Cindy's sister and her husband, Becky and Mark Henriksen.

Cindy's older brother Joseph was Normadeene's and my first child.

He's the namesake of Normadeene's father, a great honor, and an expression of love on our part. Albert Joseph was born on September 7, 1949 in Clarion, Iowa.

In the early years of ministry I found myself being more concerned about what people thought of me as a preacher and disciplinarian than being a sensitive, caring, loving father who was concerned about the deep and tender feelings that were in Joseph's heart. Joseph was a very sweet and loving tenderhearted little boy. He grew up to be a fine Christian man, an excellent, faithful husband and loving father. He married Beth Jones, whom he met while they were students at Lincoln Christian College. I had the privilege of sharing with Beth's father the officiating of their wedding. God brought two beautiful daughters into their marriage, Emily and Anna.

We thank God daily for bringing Beth and Joseph together. Beth is a multitalented person. She has a voice like an angel, and has used it for God's glory and honor through the years. She is an excellent housekeeper and a gourmet cook. Joseph has been a minister of the Gospel, for over twenty years, and a pastor in the Evangelical Orthodox Church. He has his master's degree in pastoral counseling. He is also one of Normadeene and my favorite speakers, as God gave him the gift of communication.

I believe I should share an interesting experience that took place on Halloween, 1964. Joseph, then fifteen years old, asked me for candy as he was going to have some friends over that evening. He decided to do that rather than go out for trick-or-treats. Because I received my paycheck on the first of each month, by the end of the month I was usually dead broke. I told him I would get some candy for him, fully intending to borrow a dollar from my good friend Howard Hayes, who always had money in his pocket. He was a very frugal man. I used to joke when he took a buffalo nickel out of his pocket, it would blink to see the light. I arrived at the college early and went through the day teaching my classes. I locked my office door and headed back home. As I drove down the four-lane highway through Robbinsdale, it hit me. I had forgotten about the promise I made to Joseph, and worse than that I forgot to borrow a dollar from Howard.

Panic hit me. Because I was gone so much, I was trying hard to maintain a closer relationship with Joseph than I had in the past. One thing we learned from experience is that it is very important to be true to your word with your children. I knew the candy was important to him. I was driving down a highway that was separated by a median. As I approached a stop light, I prayed, "Dear Lord, help me to get a dollar, as I need it very badly right now!" As I prayed that prayer, I was right at the stop light. The light turned yellow. The traffic behind me had to stop.

As I went through the intersection, a gust of wind blew some leaves across the road in front of me. To my surprise, there in the middle of those leaves was a dollar bill. It looked large. I stopped the car. I chased down the dollar, got back into the car and went on my way. It was an old, water-soaked dollar. I used it to buy Joseph's candy. I hadn't had a prayer answered so fast since my experience with the motorcycle angel (when I prayed for a ride to Los Angeles while I was in the Navy).

I have enjoyed sharing with you the experiences I had during the first half of my life that proved to be "Worth Any Sacrifice." It takes in approximately forty years of my life. I am convinced that any sacrifices we may have made during the first half were mainly to prepare us for the second half. I am now closer to eighty than seventy.

I say this because of the conclusion I have come to when people often ask me, "Why do bad things happen to good people?" My reply is as follows: There are four reasons bad things happen to good people. (1) Bad things happen to good people if we violate God's natural or Spiritual laws. Galatians 6:7,8 makes that clear. (2) Bad things happen to good people as in the case of Job. God may be testing our faith.

(3) Sometimes we do not know why bad things happen. However, we do know that God can take our bad times and turn them into good times. Romans 8:28 and I Corinthians 10:13 assure us of that. (4) But, as suggested above, I am convinced that the sacrifices we are called upon to make are often meant to prepare us for a very special mission in the future.

The story is told of an elderly lady who asked her minister to have her funeral and gave him instructions to follow. She said, "I want two things to be buried with me, my Bible and a fork." The minister responded with dismay, and he asked the reason for the second part of her request. She explained to him how at her church they had special potluck dinners. She said that someone would come by and tell her to save her fork, for the best was yet to come. She said that meant the dessert, not just ordinary dessert, but the special things like apple pie, chocolate cake, etc. She went on to tell the minister that when she dies, she wanted to let people know that the best was yet to come!

As I suggested above, I have enjoyed sharing the first half of my life with my readers. However, the next half includes even greater sacrifices, but much greater rewards, as we will share with you "Angels in Africa." Yes, indeed, the best is yet to come.

*The following award was given to Dr. Gibson by Minnesota Bible College on November 9, 2001.*

# A Tribute to Gerald A. Gibson

## Alumni Distinguished Service Award

### 2001

A statement in Ecclesiastes 9:10 describes our nominee for the Alumni Distinguished Service Award. "Whatever your hand finds to do, do it with all your **might**, for in the grave where you will go there is neither working, or planning nor knowledge nor wisdom." We cannot think of another person whom the sage may have had in mind. This nominee exudes power, vision, daring and optimism. It is a part of his "psyche," his whole being, his heart, his will. He is a servant of God and one who knows no discouragement, no failure, no lack of heart and vigor. He is one who cannot imagine a goal that is impossible, indeed he doesn't seem to have that word in his vocabulary. Whether young or old, educated or unlearned, a ruler or downcast, he knows no difference and sees all as they "for whom Christ died."

**Gerald A. Gibson** was born in Jacksonville, Florida, but went to high school in Excelsior, Minnesota. He spent eighteen months on the island of Guam in the Navy during World War II. He later attended San Bernardino Valley College in southern California. He was an avid golfer and served as the captain of the college team and won a golf championship. After conversion in the Central Christian Church of San Bernardino, California he came to Minnesota Bible College and earned a B.A. degree in 1950. He later studied at Lincoln Christian College, where he earned the

M.Th. degree and completed residency for his D.Th. degree. He holds an honorary doctorate from Mid-South Christian College in Memphis, Tennessee. He is married to Normadeene Pletcher of Clarion, IA. They have four children; Gibby, G.A., Cynthia and Becky. In 1955 he became professor of Old Testament for Minnesota Bible College and remained for thirteen years. During that time he established a campus ministry at the University of Minnesota and served on the staff of the dean of students of the university as a religious adviser.

In 1967–68 he was on sabbatical from MBC and helped establish Ghana Christian College and Seminary in Ghana, West Africa. While there he also helped in establishing a Christian college in Liberia, Africa. After his tenure with MBC he became the director of Campus Ministries at University of Illinois and established a chapter of the Fellowship of Christian Athletes and received permission from the Illinois Board of Regents to teach Old and New Testament for the University of Illinois and Lincoln Christian College. He has served churches as pastor in Minnesota, Illinois and Colorado and presently is the campus minister at the University of Colorado in Boulder. He has helped establish new churches in Minnesota and Colorado and Africa. He serves as an administrator-evangelist for World-Wide missions outreach. He also served as president of Mid-South Christian College in Senatobia, Mississippi for a time. He has always ministered to bring people to Christ, regardless of ethnic or cultural background, and has seen several hundred baptized as a result of his indefatigable faith.

Mr. Gibson has traveled extensively in Asia, Europe, Africa and America to plant the cross of Jesus on firm ground. He has endeared himself to leaders in education and government and the Church as an enthusiastic mentor. He was one of the "Seventy" who met to establish the Promise Keeper's Ministry with his longtime friend, Bill McCartney. No one can doubt his captivating commitment to the gospel and his vigorous faith. We are honored to claim him as one of our own and our nominee for the Alumni Distinguished Service Award for 2001.